CAMPAIGN 362

VIETNAM 1972: QUANG TRI

The Easter Offensive Strikes the South

CHARLES D. MELSON

ILLUSTRATED BY RAMIRO BUJEIRO

Series editor Nikolai Bogdanovic

OSPREY PUBLISHING
Bloomsbury Publishing Plc
Kemp House, Chawley Park, Cumnor Hill, Oxford OX2 9PH, UK
29 Earlsfort Terrace, Dublin 2, Ireland
1385 Broadway, 5th Floor, New York, NY 10018, USA
E-mail: info@ospreypublishing.com
www.ospreypublishing.com

OSPREY is a trademark of Osprey Publishing Ltd

First published in Great Britain in 2021

A catalog record for this book is available from the British Library.

ISBN: PB 9781472843395; eBook 9781472843371; ePDF 9781472843388;
XML 9781472843364

21 22 23 24 25   10 9 8 7 6 5 4 3 2 1

Maps by Bounford.com
3D BEVs by Paul Kime
Index by Angela Hall
Typeset by PDQ Digital Media Solutions, Bungay, UK
Printed and bound in India by Replika Press Private Ltd.

Artist's note

Readers may care to note that the original paintings from which the color
plates in this book were prepared are available for private sale. All
reproduction copyright whatsoever is retained by the publishers. The artist
can be contacted at the following email address:

ramirobujeiro@yahoo.com.ar

The publishers regret that they can enter into no correspondence upon
this matter.

Osprey Publishing supports the Woodland Trust, the UK's leading woodland
conservation charity.

To find out more about our authors and books visit
www.ospreypublishing.com. Here you will find extracts, author
interviews, details of forthcoming events and the option to sign up for
our newsletter.

Author's acknowledgments

Appreciation is given to Jon Hoffman of the US Army Center for Military
History, Sheon Montgomery of the Vietnam Center and Archive, Texas Tech
University, the Institute for Military History Hanoi, and the USMC Advisor's
Association. Help came from subject matter experts and collectors CSM
(Ret) Michael N. Martin, Maj (Ret) Edward J. Wages, and MSgt (Ret) Daniel K.
Whitton with uniform and equipment contributions. Photographs from the
author's collection include those provided by Capt E.W. Besch, LCdr F.C.
Brown, Col P. DeVries, 1stSgt J.D. Evans, CSM M.N. Martin, Col J.W. Ripley,
and LtCol G.E. Strickland.

A note on Vietnamese names

Vietnamese names are usually composed of three elements appearing in
order; first, the family or clan name; second, the middle name; and third,
the given name. A given name does not have to be the same for every
member of a family and some are composed of two names only.

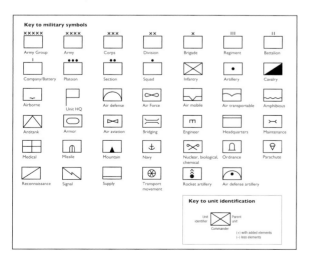

CONTENTS

North Vietnamese invasion of South Vietnam, 1972

Legend:
- Base areas
- Main attacks
- Secondary attacks

0 — 50 miles
0 — 50km

N

Demilitarized Zone (DMZ)

Dong Ha
Quang Tri
Tchepone
Hue
Infiltration routes
Da Nang
Hoi An
LAOS
I CORPS
Chu Lai
Chavane
Quang Ngai
THAILAND
Ho Chi Minh Trail
Attacu
Dak To
Kontum
Siem Pang
Pleiku
Infiltration routes
Qui Nhon
II CORPS
Tuy Hoa
CAMBODIA
Mekong River
Tonle Sap
Infiltration routes
Kratie
Nha Trang
Phum Krek
Loc Ninh
Phnom Penh
An Loc
Da Lat
Svay Rieng
Tay Ninh
III CORPS
Infiltration routes
Bien Hoa
Sihanouk Trail
Saigon
Phan Tiet
Tan Chau
Cao Lanh
My Tho
Vung Tao
Rach Gia
Can Tho
IV CORPS
Gulf of Thailand
South China Sea
Quan Long (Ca Mau)
South China Sea

ORIGINS OF THE CAMPAIGN

The US Marine Corps established and assisted several analogous services in the Far East during the Cold War (1945–91). With the conflict in Vietnam, US Marine "advisors" were present from 1954 through 1975. While engaged in a counter-insurgency war, a conventional division-size force was built that had a trial by fire during the 1972 Easter Offensive. After a decade of low-intensity conflict, the Marines had to oppose a cross-border combined-arms invasion. Critical to this was the loss and subsequent recovery of Quang Tri City. How did these Marines respond, and was their approach justified in the end? This account of the Vietnamese Marine Corps (VNMC) and its 1972 fight for the capital of Quang Tri Province will tell this tale. It is based on primary sources and published narratives. This is not a comprehensive review of the war, the VNMC, or the USMC advisory effort, which can be found in the official histories of the Vietnam War produced by the US Marine Corps, Army, Air Force, and Navy.

The period after World War II saw a number of associated Marine Corps established in the Republic of China, the Republic of Korea, the Republic of Vietnam, the Philippines, Indonesia, and Thailand. The early Cold War witnessed this proliferation of amphibious forces in Asia, in part because of the reputation the US Marines had earned in the cross-Pacific drive against Japan and in other post-war confrontations. In addition, other Marines from the Netherlands, France, and Great Britain were present at various times. These formed, with the help of foreign military aid, to fight the various conflicts to contain communist expansion in the region. This account has a particular focus on one of these, the Vietnamese Marine Corps. By way of introduction, let us start at the beginning.

In 1954, a scattering of riverine commandos called the "Marine Infantry" of the Republic of Vietnam Navy became known as the Vietnamese Marine Corps (VNMC, or *TQLC* for *Thuy Quan Luc Chien*). The Marine Corps became part of the armed forces general reserve and was separated from the Vietnamese Navy (VNN) in 1965; from then, it answered only to the Joint General Staff of the Republic of Vietnam Armed Forces (RVNAF). It expanded from a solitary battalion to nine infantry battalions and three artillery battalions in a multi-brigade structure along with service and support units. Also present was a small advisory team of US Marines as part of the Cold War proliferation of Corps of Marines in the area of the US Pacific Command. Americans brought with them a background based on established naval amphibious forces, division-level employment, and a legislated structure. Because of this, a vision of a Vietnamese Marine Division

OPPOSITE
The NVA launched the cross-border attack from neighboring sanctuaries in North Vietnam, Laos, and Cambodia using combined arms teams on a communist-bloc model. Naval and air forces remained in defense of North Vietnam proper. Surprise, along with local superiority in numbers and firepower, ensured initial success.

A Vietnamese Marine patrol using a SSB (Dong Nai swimmer support boat) in the Mekong Delta in 1965. Operations early in the war stressed the riverine and amphibious expertise needed in III and IV Corps. (USMC)

resulted that reflected the organization and doctrine that they had. This was a vision fostered by Vietnamese attendance at Marine Corps schools and the material support of the advisory effort. Despite resistance from the command structures of the Army of the Republic of Vietnam (ARVN) and US Military Assistance Command, Vietnam (USMACV), from 1968, the goal of a full division of Marines was a priority for Lieutenant-General Le Nguyen Khang, the VNMC commandant, and his advisors. It was promoted by the American policy of "Vietnamization" from 1969, which called for the Vietnamese to fight on their own. Divisional strength was met in 1970, but no large-scale employment occurred. The pressure for this increased with external operations in Cambodia in 1970 and Laos in 1971. The full division took the field for the first time in 1972 with the Quang Tri battles.

For more than a decade, decisions by three US presidents (Kennedy, Johnson, and Nixon) transformed America's role in Southeast Asia and Vietnam. Reaching a maximum troop level of 549,000, the US Armed Forces found themselves involved in a long and unpopular war. With the Nixon Doctrine from July 1969, the US began its essential disengagement from Vietnam. The United States would meet treaty commitments, but expected South Vietnam to assume the greater portions of its own defense through a policy of Vietnamization. Offensive incursions into neighboring countries of Cambodia in 1970 and Laos in 1971 indicated that there were major limitations to this policy without direct American combat support. It was a war whose continued prosecution carried on throughout Vietnam and Southeast Asia, from the Pacific region, and even the continental United States. For Americans in the Western Pacific (WestPac), Vietnam was the war that would not end. Officially known as the Ceasefire Campaign, this period is better known for the central event of the time, the Spring or Easter Offensive in South Vietnam.

The United States and Free World forces were withdrawing from South Vietnam by the early 1970s from the policy envisioned by the Nixon administration, which had the Vietnamese conduct the war with US advice and support. The total number of Americans dwindled to around 69,000. For example, after 1971, with the departure of the major US air and ground units from Military Region 1 (MR 1, formerly I Corps Tactical Zone, or I CTZ), only a residual force of Americans in the form of advisors, communicators, fire-support coordinators, and security guards remained.

The RVNAF had 1,092,087 men under arms at the time. These ranged from local militias—Provincial forces (PFs) and Regional Forces (RFs)—to the navy (VNN), air force (VNAF), and the 441,829-man ARVN. An example of the success resulting from American advice and support was the 13,462 men of the VNMC. A major challenge to the Free World strategy and efforts took place in 1972, and a critical look at the events of the fight for Quang Tri City brings together all the details of the Vietnamese Marines and their US Marine advisors' major battle honor. For South Vietnamese and American Marines, this began with confronting head-on the invading North Vietnamese along the demilitarized zone in conventional fighting that culminated with the loss of the province. During the North Vietnamese Spring Offensive, the ARVN 3d Division was defeated in a series of engagements that climaxed on May 1, 1972 with the loss of the provincial capital (known as the First Battle for Quang Tri City). The aftermath of this event was muddied by rancorous disputes among American and Vietnamese forces over the conduct of the defense of Quang Tri Province in MR 1, which saw the US Army advisors withdraw while US Marine advisors remained with their Vietnamese counterparts. After confused fighting in April and May, this singular defeat was redeemed in September with a singular victory (the Second Battle for Quang Tri City).

In 1965, Captain W.H. Bond and Captain Do Dih Vuong check the field of fire of a light machine gun. The relationship between the two was characteristic of the hands-on approach taken by US Marines from previous small war experience. (USMC)

The combat, so late in the war, was significant. For the South Vietnamese, it meant they could not hold their own against the North Vietnamese without critical American support. For the Americans, it was a foretaste of the impact of high-tempo conventional operations after an era of counter-insurgency. This and the lessons of the 1973 October or Yom Kippur War in the Middle East were important in preparing US armed forces for the 1990–91 Gulf War in Southwest Asia and elsewhere. As one participant claimed, it was a "time of change in modern warfare."

DEVELOPMENT OF THE VNMC, 1954–75

Three Marine Corps fought together in Vietnam from 1965 through 1973. Each of these were similar formations, but with their own history and traditions: the Vietnamese Marines, the United States Marines, and the Republic of Korea Marines. Common to each was a reputation for toughness on themselves and any enemy, strong unit pride, and loyalty with a privileged place within the defense structure of their respective countries.

When the French departed Indochina, they left behind the fledgling armed forces of the Republic of Vietnam. Included were the riverine forces of the navy and an assortment of army commandos that had provided the troops for them. They had formed the river assault divisions (Dinassauts) that historian Bernard B. Fall observed as "one of a few worthwhile contributions" to military tactics of the First Indochina War (1945–54). These were constituted by the French Navy to support land operations with a mix of amphibious transport, fire support, and command landing craft of various types. They would consist of anything from 12 to 20 vessels and up to two companies of commandos. Fall lamented these were disbanded because "the French had invented them and there was no equivalent in American manuals." This proved not to be the case.

The residual commandos were recovered and grouped at Nha Trang with the separation of Vietnam into north and south, and the mixed units were designated as Marine Infantry.

President Ngo Dinh Diem signed a decree that specified:

> Article 1) Effective October 1, 1954 there is created within the naval establishment a corps of infantry specializing in the surveillance of waterways and amphibious operations on coast and rivers, to be designated as: "The Marine Corps"
> …
> Article 3) The Marine Corps shall consist of various types of units suited to their functions and either already existing in the Army or Naval forces or to be created in accordance with the development plan for the armed forces.

Included as well was the inherent mission "to conduct amphibious operations to assist in the counter-insurgency effort." In April 1956, it became known as the Marine Corps of the Navy consisting of a Marine Group of two battalion landing teams.

With the Geneva Agreement that arranged the withdrawal of France from Indochina and the partition of Vietnam pending elections, the Americans moved to assist the government of South Vietnam against the communist bloc-supported People's Republic of Vietnam. By 1960, the date on the Vietnam Campaign Medal, a state of armed conflict existed between the two Vietnams and their allies with the Second Indochina War. This was a civil war that had international connotations between several world powers and their clients. It was a confrontation that displayed a full spectrum of violence, from individual terrorist acts and guerrilla fighting to conventional land combat, with extensive sea and air components. Enemy forces ranged from National Liberation Front (NLF) or VC (Vietnamese Communist) guerrillas in South Vietnam of varying quality and quantity, to the regulars of the People's Army of Vietnam (PAVN), who infiltrated into South Vietnam along the Ho Chi Minh Trail. They also defended North Vietnam with conventional combined armed forces. The Vietnamese Marines knew that: "Our country has 2,000km of coastline and an interlaced river system. As the infiltrations and sabotages of the VC increase seriously day by day, our Armed Forces are required to have a strong landing force ready to attack the enemy at any place, at any time, and at any price."

Vietnamese Marines and advisors leave an American transport vessel in the early 1960s as part of an amphibious landing exercise. Shown are the variety of weapons, uniforms, and personal equipment used at the time. (USMC)

Vietnamese Marine Corps influence increased in part with the role it played in complex national government that saw them involved in political coups in 1960, 1963, 1964, 1965, and 1966. This continual balancing of power was reflected in assignment of forces, commanders, and even the direction of the war. In 1961, the Vietnamese Marines became part of the Republic of Vietnam's armed forces general reserve. Expansion resulted from successful employment against various dissidents and bandits, which led to the organization of a 5,000-man Marine Brigade in 1962. The formation of its own training and

The political–military nature of the RVNAF saw Marines taking part in various coups throughout the 1960s. Marines and tanks secure the Gia Long Palace as the armed forces support the generals who overthrew President Diem and his family. American advisors were not involved themselves in internal politics. (*Marine Corps Gazette*)

replacement centers allowed the Marines to keep up to strength without relying on the army for manpower. According to a senior Marine advisor, "When they finish their 10-week recruit training at [Thu Duc], they are physically and psychologically toughened to handle the job." Both officers and men attended schools in the United States and specifically at Quantico, VA, where a generation of Vietnamese and Americans met and served together. Vietnamese Marine commandant Lieutenant-General Le Nguyen Khang observed that his men were proud "to be associated in spirit and deed with the select group of professional military men of many nations who call themselves Marines." They developed their own distinctive capabilities and stated: "The Marine Corps differs from friendly combat branches in the technical point of amphibious operations. Its special mission is to move by junk [local watercraft], land on unfamiliar coastal zones, speedily fight and capture bases located along the coast, establish beachheads to rapidly advance landwards and withdraw. Moreover, there are techniques relative to embarkation, debarkation, net climbing, heliborne transportation, etc. The units must thoroughly know those special points."

The Southeast Asia theater of operations divided into North Vietnam, South Vietnam, the Tonkin Gulf littoral, and inland frontiers with Laos and Cambodia. South Vietnam consisted of political provinces grouped together into military regions or tactical zones numbered Corps I, II, III, and IV (Military Regions 1, 2, 3, and 4) from the north to the south. The country was divided geographically from east to west into a coastal plain, a piedmont region, and the central highlands. A Vietnamese Marine officer described the tactical terrain faced by him and his advisors:

> If you work in the I or II Corps area, you may have the chance to climb high mountains with thick vegetation, where, in the dry season, the water problem is of more concern than the enemy. In the rainy season the water level rises considerably and currents become tremendously strong. You can send a squad patrol across a stream and a couple of hours later, this squad on returning, will find the same stream turned into a raging river. In the III Corps you may become familiar with the Rung Sat, a wet and sticky, muddy area, covered

with heavy mangroves and laced with innumerable streams, many of which are not shown on your map. If you work in the IV Corps, you may be in U Minh forest, an inundated and muddy terrain with thick vegetation where the water, red and dirty, rises permanently around your waist, and you will have no chance to see the sun except as weak and indistinct light which is what "*U Minh*" means.

As part of the national reserve, the Vietnamese Marines found themselves in action from the 17th Parallel Demilitarized Zone (DMZ) in the north to the islands of the extreme south. When assigned to a specific corps area, the Marines would serve under ARVN general officers, and the corps commanders. The narrative here deals with operations highlighted in VNMC and US Marine Advisory Unit historical materials. Before 1965, most operations were by single companies or battalions in III and IV corps. In most cases, battalions split into two task organizations (each of two reinforced rifle companies), one under the battalion commander and the other under his deputy. A variety of counter-insurgency operations were engaged in, to include search and destroy, search and clear, helicopter or riverine assault, and security tasks (civic action, area and road control, harvest protection). Characteristic employment was in response to critical situations requiring rapid movement with short notice. For example, in 1963 there were four battalion-size amphibious assaults, numerous raids and river landings, frequent helicopter movements (one of which was conducted at regimental strength), and two major air transport movements (including artillery). In hostile areas for three out of every four days of a year, the Marines "developed into an elite, tough, experienced combat force." According to the Marine advisors: "Throughout its history, it has been a fighting Marine Corps and it will continue to be until the communist Viet Cong are defeated."

Of the total of 565,350 South Vietnamese in the ARVN armed forces in 1965, only 6,500 were Marines. By then, the Vietnamese Marine Brigade was organized into a Corps headquarters, two task force headquarters ("A" and "B"), five infantry battalions, an artillery battalion, and supporting units for signals, engineers, motor transport, military police, medical, and reconnaissance. Headquarters were located in Saigon with outlying facilities at Thu Duc and Vung Tau. A colonel, who was dual-hatted as a service and brigade commander, was the commandant of the Marine Corps. By this time, Vietnamese Marines were separated from the VNN and answerable to the RVNAF high command. Present was an advisory unit from the USMC with advisors down to the unit level.

In the Rung Sat Special Zone, a river patrol craft (RPC) picks up a Marine unit from the swampy shoreline. These "local watercraft" provided mobility in otherwise impassible terrain. (Author's collection)

The command history recorded: "The Marine Brigade is used in amphibious operations and coastal operations to occupy inland objectives and to destroy the enemy; however, in recent years, the Marine Brigade has participated in ground operations much more than in amphibious operations." This required other services—armor, artillery, naval gunfire, and air support—to succeed. After 1965, the Marines deployed to the II and I Corps areas as the war progressed away from the Delta and Capital regions. Multiple battalion operations became the norm through the use of task force headquarters. Two battalions under Task Force A concluded a series of operations over a four-month period that resulted in 444 communists killed and another 150 taken prisoner. This included a notable engagement in April 1965 near An Thai, Binh Dinh Province, which resulted in the 2d Marine Battalion earning a US Presidential Unit Citation for a successful fight against a superior communist force with counter-attacks "which swept the advancing foe before them by bayonet and small-arms fire." To the Americans, this battle clearly demonstrated that a trained, disciplined Vietnamese unit with determination and leadership could defeat "hard-core" VC units of superior numbers, and that the VNMC was such a unit.

In a remarkable incident, the Vietnamese Marines recognized a unit's psychological success that occurred without a shot being fired in anger. In September 1965, Task Force A was in operations with the ARVN 23d Division northeast of Ban Me Thout, Darlac Province in the central highlands. An ethnic minority village was identified and approached by two Marine battalions. The 4th Marine Battalion was to assault a Drao village and its local FULRO militia, when the battalion commander decided to rush in using bayonets only and the shouts of "Drop your guns, drop your guns, we have no reason to fight one another."[1] As a result, the villagers did not fire, capitulated, and turned in their weapons. As such, not all Marine victories were the result of combat.

By 1966, the Marines formed its sixth infantry battalion and realigned supporting units to become a more balanced combined arms force. It still

A South Vietnamese surrender leaflet showing a Vietnamese Marine and an NVA soldier that indicated capture and survival were possible for those changing sides. For the Vietnamese, this was a civil war with international components. (Author's collection)

---

1   FULRO is an acronym for the *Front Unifié de Lutte des Races Opprimées* (United Front for the Liberation of Oppressed Races).

More often, Vietnamese Marine combat units deployed in the field against a variety of insurgent threats, often at short notice and in difficult conditions as part of the national reserve. They "punched above their weight" for the VNMC's size as a military service. (USMC)

lacked armor, aircraft, and full logistic support. From 1966 through 1967, the Marines spent more time in I CTZ and conducted operations in conjunction with the Americans in this critical location. In another episode, on June 29, 1966, a road convoy of the 2d Marine Battalion was ambushed by an estimated battalion of VC while moving from Hue City to Dong Ha in I CTZ. The battalion commander was killed and his executive officer was pinned down by fire, leaving a company commander and his advisor to assume command. A reaction force was organized while artillery and air strikes were called that turned the rout into success. The battalion lost 42 dead and 96 wounded in action, but its aggressive response killed 161 VC.

From July 30, 1967, the 3d and 4th Marine battalions participated with the ARVN 7th Division and the US 9th Infantry Division in Operation *Coronado*, the war's largest joint operation in the Mekong Delta. Landing at dawn, the Marines found themselves in the middle of a VC base camp. Machine-gun fire forced the landing site to be shifted, and fire was so heavy that resupply helicopters could not land: supplies were pushed out while airborne. Advised by the II Field Force Commander, US Army Major-General Frederick C. Weyand, to pull back and use air support to reduce the enemy, the Marine commander responded: "If we try to break contact, the Viet Cong will get away." Weyand recalled, "I was very proud of them," as the Marines advanced and killed 145 communists. In December 1967, Major Pham Nha, commanding the 5th Marine Battalion, was probing a canal in the Mekong Delta with the US Navy. When he felt the use of fire support would cause him to fall back and wait, he "ordered the boats into the heaviest fire." Along with the belated efforts of two US Army battalions and their firepower, the battalion quickly enveloped the enemy. The Marines killed 238 and captured 15 of the enemy force.

In January 1968, the Marines deployed in the Capital Military District, and in II, III, and IV CTZs as the Tet Offensive was underway. During the offensive, the Marines fought in both Saigon and Hue to defeat the communist attempt at a general uprising. Rushed to Saigon, in the first ten days of the year they killed 361 communists and captured 175 weapons. When the situation in Hue City became critical, a task force headquarters, and the 1st and 5th Marine battalions were flown to Phu Bai in I CTZ and then reinforced the Hue Citadel on February 13. The 4th Marine Battalion arrived on February 16 and for the next 12 days battled to the southwest wall, killing 618 communists, capturing 291 weapons, and suffering 518 casualties. Other fighting continued, when on September 20 the 1st Marine Battalion was attacked at Phuoc Tom. After multiple attacks, by dawn some 125 VC bodies were counted, three were captured alive, and 34 weapons were recovered for a loss of 53 Marine casualties. Recognition came in the form of a US Presidential Unit Citation for the Marine Task Force, 1st, 2d, and 4th Marine battalions and a US Army Valorous Unit Award for the 5th Marine Battalion. During this year, the Vietnamese Marines maintained a casualty-to-kill ratio of 1:7. It was noted that Marines were in the field 75 percent of the time, then the highest figure obtained by South Vietnamese forces. On October 1, 1968, a Marine Division was formed consisting of two brigades (A and B) and supporting units.

In March 1969, the 5th Marine Battalion earned a US Navy Unit Citation for action near Bien Hoa, Bien Hoa Province. This was the location of the III Corps headquarters and a major airbase. From 0300hrs, March 26, the battalion was attacked through to the next day. The fighting was so close that artillery and air strikes could not be used. The result was 173 communists killed, 20 taken prisoner, and weapons captured, for Marine losses of 24 casualties. By then, it was felt by its leaders and its advisors that: "The Vietnamese Marine Corps has truly grown into an effective combat arm in its short fifteen years of existence. Four army level citations are eloquent proof of the courage, combat experience and the determination to win of the Vietnamese Marines."

In 1970, three Marine brigades (designated 147, 258, 369), nine infantry battalions (1st through 9th), and three artillery battalions (1st, 2d, 3d) were organized, making up the Marine Division.[2] These would take part in the aggressive South Vietnamese external operations that coincided with the American departure: Cambodia in 1970, and Laos in 1971. Between April and July 1970, a series of armored and infantry operations occurred launched from II, III, and IV CTZs, initially involving some 15,000 (over time expanding from 30,000 to 50,000 troops) ARVN and American or Allied forces into the "Parrot's Beak" and "Fishhook" salients against VC and NVA base areas. Captured were 9,000 tons of weapons, ammunition, or supplies and another 7,000 tons of rice. For the Vietnamese Marines this involved Operation *Tran Hung Dao IX* in May along the Mekong River, with Brigade B at Neak Luong. Brigade A followed at Prey Veng. "The Marines completed a successful incursion into Cambodia," according to VNMC Colonel Hoang Tich Thong:

> The NVA, who had used Eastern Cambodia as a springboard to launch attacks on South Vietnam, had to retreat north to the Cambodian–Laotian border. The Cambodian Brigade, newly formed and inexperienced, were at least set in key positions. Though the Vietnamese withdrew, South Vietnam and the U.S. still supported General Lon Nol's stand against the ever-increasing Khmer Rouge, which was backed by China. The incursion gained security for III and IV Corps. The enemy no longer launched large-scale attacks in the RVN. Only unremarkable skirmishes persisted. The peace lasted until 1972, when the NVA launched a massive attack on Quang Tri Province in I Corps.

But the communist Central Office for South Vietnam (COSVN) headquarters was not eliminated. South Vietnamese and Allied casualties were balanced against a large amount of material and personnel losses inflicted on the communist side.

---

2 Infantry battalion nicknames were as follows: 1st, Wild Bird; 2d, Crazy Buffalo; 3d, Sea Wolf; 4th, Killer Shark; 5th, Black Dragon; 6th, Sacred Bird; 7th, Black Tiger; 8th, Sea Eagle; and 9th, Mighty Tiger. Artillery battalion nicknames were: 1st, Lightning Fire; 2d, Sacred Arrow; and 3d, Sacred Bow.

The entry into Laos took place between February and March 1971, with less spectacular results for the Allies. This time some 10,000 South Vietnamese, supported by Americans from I Corps, took on an estimated 25,000–30,000 NVA in an effort to cut the Ho Chi Minh Trail. Two Marine brigades—147 and 258—entered Laos, eventually occupying Fire Support bases Delta and Hotel. The third, Brigade 369, remained as reserve in South Vietnam at Khe Sanh combat base. The resulting Allied casualties and material losses were not exceeded by those of the enemy, and the South Vietnamese withdrew under pressure early (the Marine Division lost 335 dead, 768 wounded, and 37 missing in action). The Laotian incursion was the first time a Marine division command post took the field to control maneuver units. Operations advisor Major John G. Miller recalled:

> The strategy behind *Lam Son 719* called for the creation of a string of helicopter-supported firebases to protect the flanks of the main armored advance along Route 9 from South Vietnam's Khe Sanh Plateau to the principle objective, the village of Tchepone, a point on the Ho Chi Minh Trail lying some 22km inside Laos. Severing the trail would deny the enemy in South Vietnam vital supplies. Such heavy reliance on helicopters, however, was more appropriate to the flatter country of the Mekong Delta and Cambodia, as both the terrain and the weather became increasingly less hospitable closer to the rugged demilitarized zone at the 17th Parallel. In such surroundings, the U.S. advisors would have preferred to attack Tchepone with a near-invulnerable foot column of the ARVN divisions, supported by armor … They feared under the existing strategy, the crucial firebases would be subject to defeat in detail.

Marine Division commander Brigadier-General Bui The Lan addresses his men. (USMC)

Due to the friction that occurred with the respective VNMC and ARVN commanders, these operations deserve a closer look, which is not possible in this limited analysis. Conflict also arose between the VNMC brigade commanders and the acting division commander, Colonel Bui The Lan. From 1971, at least two Marine brigades remained in I CTZ facing the DMZ and the North Vietnamese, filling the vacuum left when the Americans moved from this region.

During 1972, the Vietnamese Marines were fully employed for the defense of the north, and at first were used piecemeal under control of the ARVN 3d Division. In the heavy 1972 fighting, some 2,455 Marines were killed in action and another 7,840 men were wounded during the same period. The Marine Division established itself as a major fighting force in the month-long battle to recapture Quang Tri City; in the process, they killed an estimated 17,819 North Vietnamese soldiers, took 169 prisoners, and captured or destroyed more than 5,430 weapons and vehicles. At the time of the ceasefire accords, the Marine Division was cited by the South Vietnamese government as an "outstanding unit" of the RVNAF.

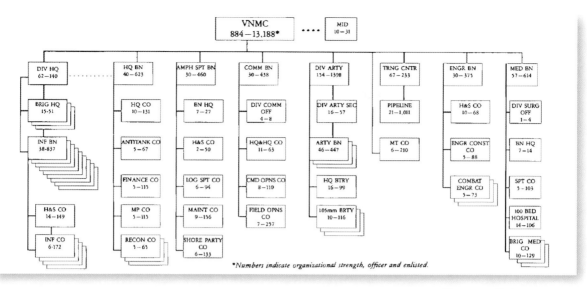

Vietnamese Marine Corps, 1972.

DEVELOPMENT OF THE US MARINE ADVISORY UNIT, 1955–73

With this background on the Vietnamese Marines, a look at the American advisory effort is in order. Lieutenant-General Le Nguyen Khang noted: "Of course no account of the Vietnamese Marine Corps would be complete without acknowledging the many contributions of the advisors from the US Marine Corps who serve with us. Their dedication to duty, valor, and sacrifices have been an inspiration to the Vietnamese Marines. Their service is indicative of the strong bonds of friendship that exist between the VNMC and the USMC." The first senior advisor, Colonel Victor J. Croizat, added: "The legacy of the French to the Vietnamese Navy is substantial; its organizational structure is essentially French in concept … The Vietnamese Marine Corps, in contrast, has been wholly a creation of the United States … the decisions that have brought them to their present status were made by the Vietnamese themselves."

From 1955 until 1961, it consisted of a lieutenant-colonel and two captains serving as the senior advisor and assistant senior advisors of the Marine Advisory Division of the Navy Section, Military Assistance and Advisory Group, Vietnam.[3] In December 1961, the organization of the advisory division expanded to include battalion-level "field" advisors for the infantry and artillery units. This provided an overall strength of eight officers and 16 enlisted Marines including a senior and assistant senior advisor (lieutenant-colonel and major), an administrative element, a logistics element, an enlisted small-unit training advisor (gunnery sergeant), four officer and enlisted infantry advisors (captains and staff sergeants), and an officer and enlisted artillery advisor (major and gunnery sergeant). By 1963, an additional small-unit training advisor was added, but the enlisted field advisors were dropped. "Upon joining the Vietnamese Marine battalions, the American advisor listens and observes. When he begins to feel that he understands what is happening and why, he offers suggestions … when asked."

3   Other US Marines served with USMACV in army, navy, and civilian advisory programs.

SENIOR MARINE ADVISORS, 1954–73

Lt-Col Victor J. Croziat	1954–June 1956
Lt-Col William N. Wilkes, Jr.	June 1956–June 1958
Lt-Col Frank R. Wilkinson, Jr.	June 1958–June 1960
Lt-Col Clifford J. Robichaud, Jr.	June 1960–August 1961
Lt-Col Robert E. Brown	August 1961–October 1962
Lt-Col Clarence G. Moody, Jr.	October 1962–October 1963
Lt-Col Wesley C. Noren	October 1963–September 1964
Col William P. Nesbit	September 1964–July 1965
Col John A. MacNeil	July 1965–July 1966
Col Nels E. Anderson	July 1966–July 1967
Col Richard L. Michael, Jr.	July 1967–July 1968
Col Leroy V. Corbett	July 1968–July 1969
Col William M. Van Zuyen	July 1969–June 1970
Lt-Col Alexander P. McMillan	June 1970–July 1970
Col Francis W. Tief	July 1970–July 1971
Col Joshua W. Dorsey III	July 1971–March 1973

Chief, Vietnamese Marine Corps Logistics Support Branch, 1973–75

Lt-Col Walter D. Fillmore	March 1973–June 1973
Lt-Col George E. Strickland	June 1973–June 1974
Lt-Col Anthony Lukeman	June 1974–April 1975

In May 1964, the advisor division transferred to the USMACV and became the Marine Advisory Unit, Naval Advisory Group, as part of an overall restructuring of American support. That year it increased in strength to 20 officers and 11 enlisted men. In December, an "on-the-job" advisor (those sent temporarily from the 3d Marine Division), Captain Donald G. Cook, was captured while with the 4th Marine Battalion in action near Binh Gia, III CTZ. He became the first US Marine taken prisoner by the communists in the conflict.[4] By January 1965, the requirement for more officer advisors resulted in another restructuring and a new strength of 25 officers, two enlisted Marines, and one navy corpsman. The senior Marine was now a colonel, in keeping with the rank of the Vietnamese commandant.

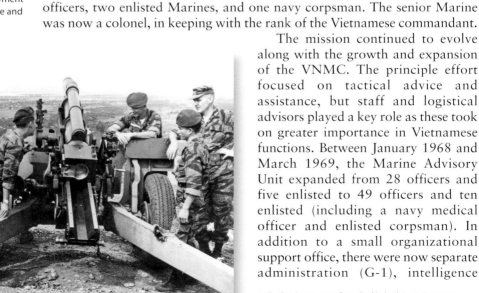

Marines with an M101 105mm howitzer, as supporting arms were part of the advisory effort for VNMC artillery battalions. Again, American equipment brought advice on employment and supply of maintenance and ammunition. (USMC)

The mission continued to evolve along with the growth and expansion of the VNMC. The principle effort focused on tactical advice and assistance, but staff and logistical advisors played a key role as these took on greater importance in Vietnamese functions. Between January 1968 and March 1969, the Marine Advisory Unit expanded from 28 officers and five enlisted to 49 officers and ten enlisted (including a navy medical officer and enlisted corpsman). In addition to a small organizational support office, there were now separate administration (G-1), intelligence

4   Declared a prisoner of war, Cook's death in 1967 was not confirmed until 1973.

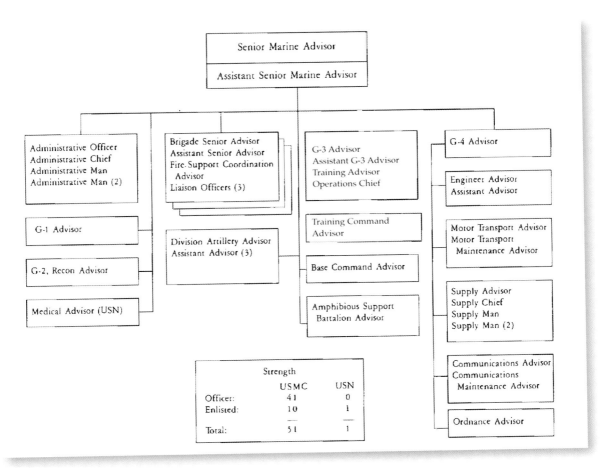

```
                    ┌─────────────────────────────┐
                    │    Senior Marine Advisor     │
                    ├─────────────────────────────┤
                    │ Assistant Senior Marine Advisor │
                    └─────────────────────────────┘
```

Administrative Officer Administrative Chief Administrative Man Administrative Man (2)	Brigade Senior Advisor Assistant Senior Advisor Fire Support Coordination Advisor Liaison Officers (3)	G-3 Advisor Assistant G-3 Advisor Training Advisor Operations Chief	G-4 Advisor
G-1 Advisor	Division Artillery Advisor Assistant Advisor (3)	Training Command Advisor	Engineer Advisor Assistant Advisor
G-2, Recon Advisor		Base Command Advisor	Motor Transport Advisor Motor Transport Maintenance Advisor
Medical Advisor (USN)		Amphibious Support Battalion Advisor	Supply Advisor Supply Chief Supply Man Supply Man (2)
			Communications Advisor Communications Maintenance Advisor
			Ordnance Advisor

Strength		
	USMC	USN
Officer:	41	0
Enlisted:	10	1
Total:	51	1

(G-2), operations (G-3), logistics (G-4), communications, and medical advisory elements. Field advisory teams existed at the brigade and battalion level (majors and captains). It should be noted that by this time in the war, a steady stream of Vietnamese Marine officers and staff non-commissioned officers had attended US Marine Corps schools and training courses in the United States. American military assistance programs saw to a dependable supply and upgrading of weapons and equipment. One deputy commandant, Colonel Nguyen Than Tri, summarized this mutual aid:

> The Vietnamese Marines are proud to be known as South Vietnam's finest fighting force, and needless to say, they never deny the unselfish contributions of the US Marine advisors coming from thousands of miles away and sharing their sacrifices. Of course, the assistance should not be superficial, but must be specified on a harmonious and sincere coordination, based on a solid friendship and relationship between two nations which are facing a common enemy: communism.

In most cases, Marine advisors were from those with a previous successful combat tour in Vietnam or with a needed technical specialty. Rank was supposed to be commensurate with those of their counterparts. Pre-deployment training varied from available Marine Corps efforts to the formal US Army Military Assistance Training Advisor (MATA) course at Fort

Bragg, NC. This five- to six-week course concentrated on language, theater orientation, physical fitness, and recent lessons learned. Then-Lieutenant W.L. Fox recalled: "We learned twenty-five words a day, Tuesday through Friday. Each morning we had a language class for three hours and used the new words." He used English at his counterpart's request, but spoke Vietnamese with his driver, radio operator, and batman. A field advisor would have three Vietnamese assigned to him: a "cowboy" aide or batman, a radio operator, and a driver. An assistant field advisor would only have the batman and radio operator. Stated the Senior Marine Advisor, "This cowboy carries your pack for you; makes your coffee in the morning; makes you a sleeping place; and guards your gear. Generally he is an all around handyman." The Vietnamese considered them "good fellows" and a "good, strong Marine who will help you with small services, and during any fighting he will be your bodyguard."

Program success was dependent upon two sources of institutional learning: guidance from the American Marine senior advisors, and the Vietnamese Marines themselves. Accordingly, the field advisors at battalion, task force, and brigade level spent 80–90 percent of their tour on operations in any of the Corps areas. Both Americans and Vietnamese agreed that a new advisor had to have his ability in combat judged before his Vietnamese counterpart would consider his advice as sound. It was added by Colonel Nguyen Than Tri: "Remember that every 12 months, maybe less because of sickness or becoming a casualty, the counterpart gets a new advisor and each one has a different way of offering advice. Then the advisor leaves again, while his counterpart, still there, keeps confronting daily, many other problems and obstacles."

A rundown of advising techniques included establishing rapport, unit assistance, approaches, attitudes, and techniques:

- Avoid giving "go" or "no go" advice, providing if possible two or three courses of action to the Vietnamese counterpart so they can adapt the best for their situation.
- Retain a sense of humor.
- Always remember the counterpart is a commanding officer.
- Do not outwardly display displeasure or disagreement with decisions which ignore the advisor's advice.
- Never boast or attempt to claim credit for advice that is implemented.
- Set a personal example of dress, bearing, industry, and initiative.
- Understand the Vietnamese point of view.
- Give the counterpart time to think over a suggestion.
- Never lose your temper.
- An advisor must be patient, persistent, and considerate.
- A "mutual admiration society" is to be avoided, as well as working outside the supply system or doing personal favors.
- Avoid interfering with internal and external politics and the Vietnamese system of discipline and officer-enlisted relations. The advisor should try to understand the system, not to change it.
- The advisor should consider that "the smile costs no money to buy, but it buys many things" and that being a know-it-all or a "sober face" would not get much of a chance to assist.

The Vietnamese concluded:

The advisor's mission and the part he must play are officially based on his professional knowledge and experience. Of course, he must possess a great deal of knowledge concerning tactics and techniques, he must know the organization of his counterpart's unit as well as his host country's customs, history, language ... Yet, he must know also the nature and character of the war that he is participating in as an advisor, the war whose front is not well-defined, the war where it is very difficult to recognize between friend and foe, the war that cannot be won by military solutions alone.

One American advisor, Captain John W. Ripley, added a moral factor:

Another remarkable result of the Marine's reputation was demonstrated over and over on the battlefield when we captured the enemy, almost always in a severely wounded state. Because our "tiger stripe" uniforms were so unique and identifiable, the enemy knew we were Marines. Never happy to be captured, they nevertheless knew they would be treated with compassion and dignity. I never once saw otherwise. Underlying this feeling of mutual respect is an incident that took place in our 5th Battalion when a patrol was overrun, resulting in the capture of 15 Marines. The enemy, knowing of the treatment their own POWs got, removed the weapons, watches, bootlaces, and other valuable equipment, and then released them. According to their Advisor, they even stated that they knew that they were Marines, and that they would not mistreat them.

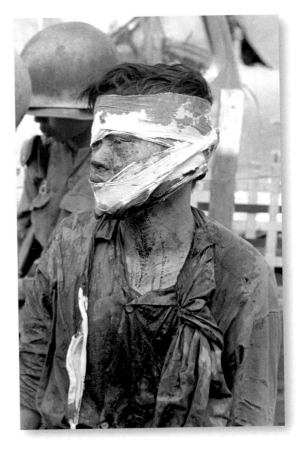

North Vietnamese Army prisoners were rare, and often in bad shape from wounds or concussion. Medical treatment was afforded at the same level as for Marines, with the added goal of useful information on the NVA units involved in the actions. (USMC)

In 1971, a US Navy Unit Commendation recognized the advisory effort: "Living side by side with their counterparts, US Marine field advisors provided sound tactical advice and enhanced Vietnamese Marine Corps combat and tactical effectiveness by coordinating and controlling all United States artillery and aircraft support." A senior advisor wrote: "They, by example and sacrifice, instilled the esprit, devotion, and confidence which have marked the combat performance of the VNMC and allowed them to take their place with pride in the international community of Marines." A reminder was posted on the wall of the advisor's Saigon head office: "The patient but persistent advisor who hears his counterpart ask, 'What do you think?' has just been informed that he is a success." This experience was not without challenges, as Vietnam historian Brigadier-General Edwin H. Simmons pointed out: "The total-immersion approach to advisory duty generally made sense to the US Marines but it was no guarantee of continuous smooth sailing, either in the field or in garrison ... stark cultural differences—embodied in the concept of "Face," in the "Commander Syndrome," and in less lofty manifestations—never could be swept aside entirely. The advisors had to become adept in getting around these problems."

The US Marine Advisory Unit receives the US Navy Unit Citation from Rear Admiral Robert S. Salzer on August 12, 1971. This was from the efforts of the previous 16 years of service. (USMC)

By 1972, the advisory effort focused primarily on training, logistics, and staff functions. In keeping with the reduction of Free World Military Forces in South Vietnam, the advisory unit was concurrently reduced and field advisors were withdrawn from the battalions and moved to the brigade level. The Easter Offensive changed this, and in May 1972, the advisory unit fully deployed all available advisors to the field in support of the Vietnamese Marine Division. It was during this period that the US Marine Advisory Unit reached its greatest strength of 67 men. As continued combat exhaustion and illness depleted this staff, in July 1972, an additional nine US Marine advisors were provided as augmentation (nine more would arrive by year's end). In addition, there was increased participation from Sub Unit One, 1st Air–Naval Gunfire Company (ANGLICO). This support of "a few Marines" contributed to the Vietnamese Marines defining fight for Quang Tri City.

Senior Marine Advisor Colonel Joshua W. Dorsey III concluded:

The advisory program initially was designed to improve the expertise of the tactical unit commander. The success of this program enabled the Marine Advisory Unit to reorient its efforts so that by early 1972, permanent battalion advisors were no longer required. At that point in time, liaison officers were provided to battalions on an as required basis for coordination of U.S. supporting arms and emphasis was primarily directed towards brigade- and division-level advice and assistance as well as technical management guidance in logistical and administrative fields. By the time of the withdrawal of the Marine Advisory Unit, the Marine Division was almost totally self-sufficient in all other areas.

Marine advisors and air–naval gunfire liaison teams provided the critical channel for air power and naval gunfire in the supporting-arms system, as with this forward observation and air control party. (USMC)

The experience of the advisory effort resonated long after the conflict concluded, including with the senior leadership of the USMC. Some 29 Vietnam-era advisors were later general officers and held key positions in subsequent conflicts through the 1990–91 Gulf War. Five were four-star generals, with two being assistant commandants of the USMC, while three were theater combatant commanders.

CHRONOLOGY

1946–54 First Indochina War: People's Republic of China supports the Vietnamese communists, United States supports the French colonial union.

1954–56 Defeat of French at Dien Bien Phu followed by the Geneva Accords; North and South Vietnam established as a provisional measure; France withdraws while America expands aid to South Vietnam.

1954, October 1 Vietnamese Marine Corps established as part of the Vietnamese Navy; first US Marine advisor assigned.

1955 US Marine Advisory Unit formed.

1959–60 North Vietnam infiltration of South Vietnam, NLF formed; South Vietnamese campaign begins with US aid, advice, and combat support.

1963 South Vietnam President Diem overthrown and murdered.

1964 Gulf of Tonkin naval incident leads to increased American involvement.

1965 Vietnamese Marine Corps separated from the Vietnamese Navy.

1965–73 Second Indochina War; Allied Free World "Big War" undertaken in support of South Vietnam; general mobilization; air and naval war against North Vietnam (Operation *Rolling Thunder*); fighting escalates in South Vietnam (1968–69), Cambodia (1970), and Laos (1971).

1971

July 9 Americans no longer to defend the DMZ at the 17th Parallel, having done so since 1966; formation of the ARVN 3d Division for this task.

November 12 President Nixon announces the American military forces will take a purely defensive stance, with offensive operations left to the South Vietnamese.

1972

January 12 Long Cheng, Laos captured by communist forces using conventional combined-arms (armor and artillery) tactics.

January 25 Presidents Nixon and Nguyen Van Thieu announce an Allied Peace Plan.

February 21 President Nixon arrives for talks in China, and changes in American Pacific strategy.

March 23 Paris Peace Talks suspended at American request.

March 30 North Vietnamese *Nguyen–Hue* Offensive begins, also known as the Vietnamese Ceasefire Campaign; Quang Tri attacked in MR 1.

April 5–7 Loc Ninh captured in MR 3, and An Loc surrounded.

April 6 Recall of US Seventh Air Force commander for unauthorized bombing strikes beyond Vietnam.

April 7 Resumed air and naval bombardment of North Vietnam with operations *Freedom Train* and *Linebacker I*.

April 15 Unrestricted bombing of North Vietnam, including Haiphong and Hanoi, authorized.

April 23 Dak To captured in MR 2.

April 27 Quang Tri City attacked in MR 1; Paris Peace Talks resume.

May 1 Quang Tri City in MR 1 captured by communists.

May 3	Bong Son in MR 2 captured by communists.
May 4	Paris Peace Talks suspended by Americans and South Vietnamese.
May 8	North Vietnam ports mined, along with an offer of withdrawal of American forces for a ceasefire.
May 14–25	Kontum in MR 2 attacked by communists.
May 19	Chinese and Soviet delegations arrive in Hanoi to increase support.
May 22	President Nixon arrives in Moscow to discuss changes in American Pacific strategy.
June 21	American troop strength in South Vietnam at 60,000.
July 13	Paris Peace Talks resume.
August 18–19	ARVN Fire Support Base (FSB) Ross captured by NVA in MR 1.
September 16	Quang Tri Citadel recaptured by ARVN forces.
September 26–27	National Security Affairs Advisor Henry Kissinger and North Vietnamese advisor Le Duc Tho conduct private talks in Paris.

October 19–20	Kissinger and Nguyen Van Thieu conduct private talks in Saigon.
October 24	*Linebacker* bombing north of the 20th Parallel is ended as peace gesture.
November 11	Direct American combat participation in South Vietnam ends.
November 20–21	Kissinger and Le Duc Tho private talks continue, but reach a standstill by December 13.
December 18–29	*Linebacker II* B-52 bombing of Hanoi continues.

1973

January 27	Paris Peace Accords signed by US and Democratic Republic of Vietnam (DRVN); prisoner exchange begins.
January 28	Allied Ceasefire Campaign ends.
February 21	Ceasefire reached in Laos.
February 25	American air operations continue from Thailand.
March 14	Sub Unit One, 1st ANGLICO deactivated.
March 29	VNMC US Marine Advisory Unit deactivated.

Senior American amphibious force leadership in 1972 included Task Force 76's Rear Admiral W.D. Toole and 9th Marine Amphibious Brigade's General E.J. Miller. Their commands provided direct support in the recapture of Quang Tri. (USMC)

OPPOSING FORCES AND COMMANDERS

NORTH VIETNAM

The PAVN (or NVA) included integrated ground, air, and naval forces, with material and technical support from the Soviet Union and the Peoples' Republic of China. North Vietnam possessed a complex of anti-aircraft artillery, missiles (including SA-2s and fire control systems), and aircraft (including MiG-21s and air control systems), along with coastal naval forces. This was actively supported by communist-bloc military and logistics advisors. Forces were organized and equipped along Soviet or Chinese lines, generally infantry heavy with excellent anti-tank, artillery, and anti-aircraft weapons to compensate for a lack of air power on the battlefield. Modern equipment included amphibious and main battle tanks, armored personnel carriers, mobile ZSU-57-2s and ZSU-23-4s, SA-7s, and AT-3s.

The communist forces divided into NVA units formed and trained in North Vietnam and People's Liberation Armed Forces (PLAF) units formed and trained in South Vietnam by the NLF, the so-called VC. Main-force units came under the command and control of Military Regions One through Four in North Vietnam and Five through Nine in South Vietnam. This included the B5 or Quang Tri Front (DMZ) and B4 Front (Laos and Route 9), also known as the Tri–Thien–Hue Military Region; B3 or Tay Nguyen Front (Central Highlands); B1 Front (Coastal Lowlands); and B2 Front (Saigon area). The VC had different designations, regions, and sub-regions under the Cambodia-based COSVN. Guerrilla or local forces were with the province, district, or village communist parties.

For VNMC units, duty in the field was common in all the military corps tactical zones, as seen with this artillery battery supporting a deployed brigade in Military Region 1. They organized into combined-arms task forces, which gave them more firepower than equivalent ARVN units had. (Author's collection)

DRVN National Command Authorities, President and General Secretary Ton Duc Thang
Party First Secretary Le Duan
Prime Minister Pham Van Dong
Chairman of Council of Ministers Nguyen Huu Tho
Minister for Foreign Affairs Nguyen Duy Trinh
Minister of Defense and Central Military Party Commission General Vo Nguyen Giap
DRVN Military High Command, Chief of General Staff Colonel-General Van Tien Dung

NORTH VIETNAMESE ORDER OF BATTLE

B5 AND B4 FRONTS: TRI–THIEN–HUE REGION
Major-General Le Trong Tan
Political Deputy Le Quang Doa[5]
Reinforced by the 27th, 31st, 126th, and 264th Infantry regiments; the 38th and 84th Artillery regiments (122mm, 130mm guns); and the 202d and 203d Armored brigades (T-54/55 or Type 59 main battle tanks, PT-76 or Type 63 amphibious tanks, BTR-50 or Type 63 armored personnel carriers). In addition, there were an estimated 59 NVA/VC maneuver companies and seven combat support units. Eventual totals in RVN MR 1 included seven infantry divisions, one anti-aircraft artillery division, with 29 separate regiments of infantry, artillery, anti-aircraft, sappers, and armor. This provided an estimated force ratio of 2:1 in MRs 1 and 2 (more so in MR 2 than MR 1, where an attack by the North appeared more likely to analysts in the South).

I Corps commander Lieutenant-General Hoang Xuan Lam, ARVN during 1972. Marines in this military region served under his command. (USMC)

NVA 70B CORPS
702d Command Group Headquarters
(based in Laos and along Route 9, with 304th, 308th, and 320th divisions)

NVA DIVISIONS
304th Infantry Division
9th Regiment
24th Regiment
66th Regiment
308th Infantry Division
36th Regiment
88th Regiment
102d Regiment
312th Infantry Division
141st Regiment
165th Regiment
209th Regiment
320B Infantry Division
48th Regiment
52d Regiment
64th Regiment
324B Infantry Division
29th Regiment
803d Regiment
812th Regiment
325th Infantry Division
18th Regiment
95th Regiment
101st Regiment
711th Infantry Division
31st Regiment
38th Regiment
270th Regiment

5   Vietnamese general officer ranks vary in time and correctness.

SOUTH VIETNAM

The Republic of Vietnam Armed Forces included autonomous ARVN, VNAF, VNN units; with material, technical, and military support from the USMACV, Seventh Air Force, and Seventh Fleet of the US Pacific Command.

As previously noted, South Vietnam distributed its forces through Corps Tactical Zones, numbered from north to south I, II, III, and IV; later renamed Miliary Regions 1 through 4. Each was commanded by a senior general officer with strong political and regional associations. This was reflected by ARVN units with ties at the local, district, and regional level. Forces were organized along US/NATO models of combined-arms teams and logistical support. Even so, the basic army division was more static and defense-oriented with a regional focus. Only the Marines, Airborne, Air Force, and Navy reflected national deployment requirements.

SOUTH VIETNAMESE ORDER OF BATTLE

RVN MILITARY REGION 1 (I CORPS), DA NANG
Lieutenant-General Hoang Xuan Lam
Lieutenant-General Ngo Quang Truong
Reinforced by 175mm guns, 155mm howitzers, 40mm and quad 12.7mm anti-aircraft weapons.
USMACV First Regional Advisory Command (FRAC)
Major-General Frederick J. Kroesen
Major-General Howard H. Cooksey

RVN DIVISIONS, BRIGADES, GROUPS
1st Infantry Division, Hue (Major-General Pham Van Phu)
1st Regiment
3d Regiment
54th Regiment
Division Artillery (105mm, 155mm howitzers)
Recon, Signal, Engineer, Medical, Supply
2d Infantry Division, Quang Ngai, Chu Lai (Colonel Phan Hoa Hiep)
4th Regiment
5th Regiment
6th Regiment
Division Artillery (105mm, 155mm howitzers)
Recon, Signal, Engineer, Medical, Supply
3d Infantry Division, Ai Tu, Da Nang (Brigadier-General Vu Van Giai, Brigadier-General Nguyen Duy Hinh)
2d Regiment
56th Regiment
57th Regiment

Division Artillery (105mm, 155mm howitzers)
Recon, Signal, Engineer, Medical, Supply
1st Armored Brigade, Da Nang (Colonel Nguyen Trong Luat, Colonel Tran Tin, Colonel Vu Quoc Gia)
4th Armored Cavalry Squadron (M41 medium tanks, M113 APCs)
7th Armored Cavalry Squadron (M41 medium tanks, M113 APCs)
11th Armored Cavalry Squadron (M41 medium tanks, M113 APCs)
17th Armored Cavalry Squadron (M41 medium tanks, M113 APCs)
20th Tank Squadron (M48 main battle tanks, M113 APCs)[6]
1st Ranger Group
Light infantry battalions, including Border Ranger Defense units of former US Civilian Irregular Defense Groups

6   Squadrons were battalion-size tank and mechanized infantry formations, with company-size troops.

Marine Division, General Reserve, Saigon (Lieutenant-General Le Nguyen Khang, Colonel/Brigadier-General Bui The Lan)
Brigade 147
Brigade 258
Brigade 369
Division Artillery (105mm howitzers)
Recon, Signal, Engineer, Medical, Supply
Airborne Division, General Reserve, Saigon (Lieutenant-General Du Quoc Dong, Brigadier-General Le Quang Luong)
Brigade 1
Brigade 2
Brigade 3
Division Artillery (105mm howitzers, airborne)
Recon, Signal, Engineer, Medical, Supply

VNMC

Organization and basing

According to the Vietnamese, "we are proud to see that our ancestors knew how to effectively organize and use landing troops. Under the Ly and Tran dynasties, landing troops had been used to conquer the country of Chiem Thanh and King Quang Trung, with marvelous tactics, brilliantly triumphed over the Thanh troops and chased them out of the frontiers of our country." Other examples were from World War II and the Korean War that confirmed the effectiveness and continued influence of the American Marines across the Pacific region.

The battalion was the primary focus of unit esprit and the paternal form of leadership that reflected Vietnamese society. Long-serving professional officers and Marines who had acquired a great deal of experience at war staffed the battalions. An infantry battalion was manned with some 36 officers and 840 men arranged in four rifle companies and a headquarters and service company. Rifle companies were numbered 1 to 4 in each battalion. A rifle company had three rifle platoons and a weapons platoon. Rifle squads comprised 13 men in three fire teams of four men each. Mortars, heavy machine guns, communications, and medical support were with the battalion headquarters. Fire support had origins with 4.2in. mortars, 75mm pack howitzers, and finally 105mm howitzers organized first as companies, batteries, and finally artillery battalions.

When possible, more than one infantry battalion was used in conjunction with a task force or brigade headquarters to provide additional support. Higher formations included the Marine Infantry Group; then from 1962, Marine Brigade Task Forces "A" and "B;" from 1970, brigades 147, 258, and 369 (reflecting battalion assignments); and in 1975 Brigade 468 was formed. Division-level units included headquarters, amphibious support, signal, medical, and engineer battalions as well as patrol, anti-tank, military police, and amphibious tractor companies.

Senior leadership, 1971–72, from the left: VNMC Commandant Lieutenant-General Le Nguyen Khang, Senior Marine Advisor Colonel J.W. Dorsey, and Commander Naval Forces Vietnam Rear Admiral Robert S. Salzer. (USMC)

The Headquarters, VNMC, was located in Saigon at the Bo Tu Lenh complex, along with the US Marine Advisory Unit. Outlying facilities were at the Thu Duc, Cuu Long Navy Base, and Vung Tau. The Marines benefited from military construction programs begun by USMACV in 1967, expanded with Vietnamization in 1969, and completed by 1971. Located 10 miles north-northwest of Saigon at Di An were the Song Than Base complex, with training center and ranges, a medical battalion and hospital, battalion base camps, dependent housing and other community services.

Personal equipment

The Vietnamese Marines that went to war in 1965 reflected knowledge of the "soldiers load," a subject that was examined critically by S.L.A. Marshall and the US Marine Corps Schools in the early 1950s. In practice, considerations of culture, circumstances, and supply were shown to have been just as important factors in determining what was carried in battle.

By then, the Vietnamese were armed with American .30 and .45-cal. small arms that had been in existence since World War II and the Korean War: M1 rifles, M1 and M2 carbines, M1911 pistols, M1A1 submachine guns, and M1918 Browning automatic rifles. This was followed by outfitting with M16s, M60s, and newer small arms by USMACV at the same time as the other South Vietnamese forces.

The Marines were a priority for this replacement along with the airborne units of the national reserve.

This required the use of webbing and accessories to carry the ammunition and magazines for these weapons. Individual combat equipment varied greatly over the period, from a mixture of French and American surplus to the standardized issue of M56 load-carrying equipment from the USMACV beginning in 1965. This included the replacement of the M44 and M45 combat and cargo packs with the theater-designed, semi-rigid indigenous rucksack, the "ARVN pack." A distinctive Vietnamese field item was the individual hammock made from parachute canopy nylon and suspension lines used with a waterproof poncho or ground sheet.

Another characteristic Vietnamese item was the ever-present squad aluminum cooking pot. This was an essential item in the way the Vietnamese troops ate while in the field. The Marines carried five days of rations of rice, dried salted fish, and canned sardines. What was not issued had to be

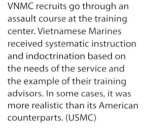

VNMC recruits go through an assault course at the training center. Vietnamese Marines received systematic instruction and indoctrination based on the needs of the service and the example of their training advisors. In some cases, it was more realistic than its American counterparts. (USMC)

acquired locally. A typical meal consisted of five types of food: one salted, one fried or roasted, vegetable soup, green vegetables, and rice. A fermented fish sauce, nuoc mam, was served as a spice and source of protein. While rice was the staff of life, Vietnamese Marines enjoyed American C-rations when they could get them, "especially ham and limas." A senior advisor observed to US Marines: "You will strictly be eating Vietnamese food when you're out on an operation. This runs about 50 piasters a day—13 bucks a month. For this you can get all the rice and nuoc mam you can eat plus all the assorted goodies." Problems resulted if the tactical situation prevented meals from being obtained and prepared. If circumstances did not allow resupply, then the Marines would go hungry. This included any American advisors that were present, most of whom lost weight with the Vietnamese in the field.

Uniforms and insignia

An examination of some of the corporeal aspects of the Vietnamese Marines and US advisors is useful for considering their performance. This was in more than just material matters because it reflected corporate tradition or myth. Specific designations and numbers used to identify clothing and equipment were complicated by different languages, although in most cases, nomenclature was just the translation of the equivalent terms, at first in French, and then for American items. There were also different designations for the same object: the jargon used by the Marines, the supply term used to catalog the item, and the manufacturer's nomenclature. The vernacular used was preferred to find a balance between regulation and reality for the period covered.

The Vietnamese Marines used naval rank insignia with equivalent army or air force rank titles. Eight enlisted grades existed and seven officer grades were used through brigadier-general. The enlisted rank structure reflected French influence, beginning with private, private first class, corporal,

Unit insignia for the Marine Brigade. (Author's collection)

corporal-chief, sergeant, sergeant-chief, adjutant, and adjutant-chief (later simplified to private, private first class, corporal, sergeant, sergeant first class, master sergeant, sergeant-major, warrant officer). The officers used the American-style candidate through second lieutenant, first lieutenant, captain, major, lieutenant-colonel, and colonel (over time, senior officers included sub-brigadier, brigadier-general, major-general). In order to avoid rank inflation, promotion was based upon experience or ability, and only to available billets: as a result, "Average time in grade for officers and NCOs cannot be stated accurately." Officers and enlisted men both wore their rank on naval-style shoulder boards. Silver braid on black was worn instead of the naval gold. In the field, this was simplified to wearing a single shoulder board on the shirt front. This resulted in a miniature version that could be fastened on a shirt or pocket button. Late in the war, miniature rank insignia embroidered in black on green cloth was worn on the collar or headgear in the American fashion. All three types of rank badges were in use throughout the war. On occasion, Vietnamese Army metal pin-back rank was worn during joint operations.

Distinctive unit emblems evolved within the service over time and defy specific documentation. The earliest emblems included Vietnamese Navy badges worn on berets and service caps. These were in metal and embroidered forms. The emblems were gold for officers and silver for enlisted men. A unique Marine Infantry badge had a much longer service life. It displayed crossed anchors within a plain circle. It was in both metal and embroidered variations. The embroidered cap badge used a dark blue and then a later green backing, depending on the beret color. The officer's version had a wreath of rice stalks around a crossed anchor central design; the enlisted version had only the crossed anchors.

American Marine advisors in Vietnamese Marine uniforms with the variety of insignia used. From left to right: Captain J.E. Johnson, Captain J.W. Ripley, Lieutenant-Colonel G.H. Turley, and Captain W.D. Wischmeyer. Again, a shared experience at odds with regulation American dress. (USMC)

VNMC command and staff list, 1972–73

Lieutenant-General Le Nguyen Khang[1]	VNMC Commandant, Division Commander
Colonel Bui The Lan[2]	VNMC Deputy Commandant
Colonel Le Dinh Que	Chief of Staff
Lieutenant-Colonel Nguyen The Luong[3]	Deputy Chief of Staff, Operations and Logistics
Colonel Pham Van Chung	Chief of Staff, Forward HQ
Lieutenant-Colonel Nguyen Nang Bao	Brigade 147
Lieutenant-Colonel Ngo Van Dinh	Brigade 258
Colonel Pham Van Chung[4]	Brigade 369
Major Tran Ngoc Toan[5]	Song Than Base
Lieutenant-Colonel Nguyen Duc An	Training Center

1. Later, Brigadier-General Bui The Lan.

2. Promoted brigadier-general May 28, 1972. Later, Colonel Nguyen Thanh Tri.

3. Later, Colonel Pham Van Chung.

4. Later, Lieutenant-Colonel Nguyen The Luong.

5. Later, Lieutenant-Colonel Le Ba Binh.

Unit insignia for the Marine Division. (Author's collection)

In 1959, a new service device was adopted with an eagle, glove, and anchor motif. It closely followed the American Marine emblem, but evolved to incorporate Vietnamese traditional features. According to official references, these included an anchor through a globe for the Marines' naval character, a five-pointed red star with the outline of Vietnam in the center indicating combat spirit and the five parts of the world, and an eagle spreading its wings to represent unyielding martial spirit. A black background stood for bravery in difficult conditions—the colors of a "death volunteer." The design eventually formed the basis for cap, beret, unit, and service insignia. Again, there were officer and enlisted versions. The metal cap and beret badge was in gold and silver for officers and in brass for enlisted Marines. The embroidered beret badge was backed in green and then later in red.

While field or combat uniforms were at first unmarked similar to the American Marines, major variations of unit and service insignia developed. Cloth emblems worn on the combat uniform were generally from a high-quality weave manufacturer. Printed variations were for general service use. First was a full-color distinctive unit insignia on a black shield worn on the upper left sleeve, indicating the Marine group or brigade. This was in line with ARVN practice. Later, a full-color VNMC emblem within a green disc was worn on the right breast pocket as a service emblem at the time additional brigades were formed. Finally, a full-color insignia on a green shield was worn on the upper left sleeve for the Marine Division, replacing the previous brigade insignia. One Marine advisor recalled that in 1967, he had the Marine brigade shoulder patch on his left sleeve, a US Marine nametape over the left chest shirt pocket, a service emblem on the right shirt pocket, along with a nametape in battalion colors.

Battalion distinctive unit insignia developed at the same time from the colored cloth nametape or tags worn over the right shirt chest pocket. These derived from the colors used to assemble units after amphibious or riverine landings. Noted in use were the following: green with white-lettered personal names for division or brigade headquarters; for the infantry, blue with black letters for 1st Battalion; purple with black letters for 2d Battalion; olive with black letters for 3d Battalion; red with black letters for 4th Battalion; black with yellow letters for 5th Battalion; green with black letters for 6th Battalion; orange with black letters for 7th Battalion; blue with red letters for 8th Battalion; and blue-grey with black letters for 9th Battalion. The artillery battalions used white and red combinations and other supporting units followed suit. The advisors added a tape over the left shirt pocket with "US MARINES" in black letters on olive green. Eventually, battalion insignia were designed and worn on the upper right sleeve based around the unique designations acquired in action. In part, this reflected the bottom-up unit esprit that existed and a sense of tribal unit identity that was both a unit strength and occasional limitation where teamwork was required. The Marines themselves were self-styled "Warriors from the Sea."

Like other Marines, the Vietnamese had a series of uniforms that reflected climate and occasion: service dress with coat, tie, and cap; khaki dress; and the combat dress that became its characteristic uniform as the war progressed. The initial combat uniform was the plain olive-green shirt and trousers used by the army. This remained in use as a basic training and fatigue uniform after the adoption of a camouflage uniform, more out of economy than sentiment. In 1956, a distinctive "sea-wave" or "tiger-stripe" camouflage pattern was adapted for combat clothing. The four-color cloth was imported and made into uniforms in South Vietnam. In general, it consisted of a shirt with two covered chest pockets, and a pair of trousers with two thigh, seat, and leg pockets. Extra pen and cigarette pockets on the shirtsleeves or trouser legs were popular modifications. There were also examples of the army leaf-pattern camouflage being used. This allowed for considerable variations in style and quality. A black web belt with solid-face brass buckle was issued, and the American Marine open-face buckle was

A comparison of uniforms seen on two Marines. On the left, an American, and the right a Vietnamese communicator in utilities, most commonly used for work or in combat. This was the precursor to universal American camouflage used after the war in Vietnam. (USMC)

Vietnamese Marine color guard on parade in Saigon for the November 1, 1972 National Day. An indicator of the national elite status of the Marines, it reflected their place as the pride of the country. Shown is a variation of the field uniform, with medals, lanyards, and the distinguishing green beret. (USMC)

favored as well. Footwear ranged from local Bata canvas boots, to full leather combat boots, or the American tropical combat or "jungle" boot. A black or dark blue navy beret and badge of the Marine Infantry were worn at first, but by 1965, standard headgear was a green beret with badge. Also worn was a utility cap "cover" or bush hat in the camouflage pattern. The M1 helmet was used with either a net or American camouflage pattern cloth cover.

A senior advisor said that: "You will be issued four sets of camouflaged equipment, or as we call them 'Tiger Suits.' You will have to buy a rain hat—these are made out of the same camouflage material. They generally run about 200 piasters [US $1 = 118 piasters]. Also a green beret which is about 600 piasters. A Vietnamese hammock which is about 500 piasters and name tags, patches and different paraphernalia you put on your tiger suits."

Field uniforms were also used on ceremonial occasions with the addition of medals or medal ribbons and unit colored neck scarves. White parade gloves, duty belts, shoulder cords, and boot laces contributed to this. The Marine Band had its own distinct variation on the theme that included a tailored uniform with the camouflaged shirt worn outside the trousers as a jacket. Fourragères on the left shoulder were added for the four classes of armed forces unit awards that existed: in red for gallantry (two or more citations), green for military merit (four or more citations), yellow for national recognition (six or more citations), and a combination of all three colors for outstanding unit recognition (nine or more citations). By 1970, the Marine battalions had received some 27 RVNAF citations. The division was recognized in 1972 with the unit color of the Gallantry Cross.

Unit awards came from both the Vietnamese and American governments for combat actions that made the VNMC a distinctive appearance in garrison and parade. Displayed are Gallantry crosses, Valorous Unit, and US Presidential Unit citations attached to unit colors. (USMC)

OPPOSING PLANS

THE PRELUDE TO DEFEAT

By 1971, with the departure of most American combat units from MR 1, VNMC brigades were deployed in rotation to Quang Tri Province and placed under ARVN command. With the incursion into Laos in February 1971, under Lieutenant-General Hoang Xuan Lam (who commanded I Corps) as part of Operation *Lam Son 719*, the Vietnamese Marines were used at brigade strength. Marine Lieutenant-General Le Nguyen Khang and his American advisors felt Lieutenant-General Hoang Xuan Lam failed to support the VNMC units, giving Lam the nickname "Bloody Hands" for his expenditure of Marine lives during the flawed incursion. The extent to which politics overrode tactical decisions was difficult to gauge when VNMC requests to withdraw had been met by ARVN comments such as "Now the Marines will have to fight." Speculation circulated that damage to the Vietnamese Marines was desired in order to weaken the General Le Nguyen Khang–Vice President Nguyen Cao Ky faction, just as the losses to the Vietnamese airborne had impacted on the General Hoang Xuan Lam–President Nguyen Van Thieu faction in the Vietnamese government. These same arguments emerged again the next year during the defense of Quang Tri. This exemplified the complex network of political, professional, and familial relations that shifted within the policies of America and Vietnam.

A more significant factor with *Lam Son 719* was that the Americans provided critical control of maneuver and fire support, which should have come from the Vietnamese. The senior American commander in Vietnam, General Creighton W. Abrams, Jr., concluded in July 1971 that the Vietnamese suffered from weak leadership and the inability to control American firepower. Abrams did not expect US advisors to "play a major role in the improvement of South Vietnamese military forces." The Vietnamese Marines learned from combat with the NVA and adjusted accordingly, and even the ARVN commanders noted the Marines had retained unit integrity regardless of losses.

USMACV's General Creighton W. Abrams, Jr. during 1972. He had to balance the needs of pacification, combat action, and American troop stand-down in the face of the surprise offensive. (USMACV)

In the fall of 1971, the ARVN 3d Division—the Ben Hai Division—was formed and used for the defense of the DMZ. Vietnamese Marine brigades assigned this area of operations came under the division's Brigadier-General Vu Van Giai for tactical matters but still remained firmly under VNMC control for material and political reinforcement. The relationship between separate military organizations was based upon the degree of support provided: general, direct, or attached. In theory, an attached unit was supposed to have the same level of consideration as one belonging to the parent command; in practice, this was often not the case. According to Major-General Frederick J. Kroesen, Jr., the senior American in MR 1, Brigadier-General Vu Van Giai was not satisfied with Marine responsiveness to his orders, but the brigades were combat tested, fully reliable, and respected. Major-General Kroesen observed that the ability of these brigades to rotate forces proved vital in maintaining combat effectiveness. Significantly, they were supplied, equipped, and maintained at effective strength well by Marine logistics and replacement channels.

Allied Free World and communist forces evaluated the experience from Laos with *Lam Son 719* and asked if the mixed results could result in future success. Within the North Vietnamese politburo there were opposing pro-Soviet and pro-Chinese factions at play over grand strategy and tactics used to achieve the unification of the two Vietnams. In effect, this was a debate over what phase of communist revolutionary warfare they were at (strategic defensive, strategic stalemate, or strategic offensive); would an unconventional people's war continue in South Vietnam, or was it now time to move to a conventional war of movement? Defensive goals in 1971–72 were still the overthrow of the existing government in South Vietnam and replacing it with a unified regime, involving building up forces in the north with holding actions in the south. But Party First Secretary Le Duan and Chief of the General Staff Van Tien Dung now articulated more active offensive goals that would destroy a number of units of the RVNAF strategic reserve, deal a significant defeat to Vietnamization, advance the efforts to defend North Vietnam, and liberate South Vietnam. The strategic initiative was passing to the north with the withdrawal of American forces and upcoming 1972 presidential elections, and had the objective of forcing the "US imperialists to negotiate an end to the war from a position of defeat." Despite American diplomatic overtures to the Soviets and Chinese, their support to the communist regime actually increased in material terms. Three locations were designated for an offensive in 1972: northern MR 1, central MR 2, and northwestern MR 3. A build-up of communist forces took place along the DMZ and the Laotian border areas west

Preparations for the communist offensive included moving units and briefing troops as to their expected goals, including this mortar unit. These were regular forces rather than guerrillas. (PAVN)

of Quang Tri and Thua Thien provinces. This included the movement of a front and corps headquarters (Tri–Thien–Hue Front, 70B Corps) and three NVA divisions (304th, 308th, and 320th). Other NVA combat forces were identified west of Pleiku.

Allied operations and intelligence staffs considered the situation at the same time as the communists. Indicators were the expansion of forces in the border areas of Laos and Cambodia, but the chances of a major offensive were considered low despite American troop withdrawals and the South Vietnamese build-up of forces to take their place. While smaller outlying outposts were subject to attack, major population areas were not threatened. Viet Cong and local forces were hindered by pacification programs being run by the Republic of Vietnam government. It was believed by the joint staffs that any communist external threats could be countered by direct attack across the DMZ, amphibious operations north of the DMZ, increased aircraft carrier operations, and covert attacks on North Vietnamese coastal areas. Business ran as usual as the end of the monsoon season approached and with it the start of campaigning opportunities during the Lunar New Year.[7] Directives from Saigon warned of the need for a high state of readiness during the Tet period. This was reinforced by a visit to Vietnam by General William C. Westmoreland, Chief of Staff of the US Army, to his former deputy General Creighton W. Abrams. Both Abrams and RVN Joint General Staff's General Cao Van Vien were confident they could handle the situation that

B-52 bombers made their impact felt on the battlefield with distinctive power. The Arc Light raids took out large swaths of enemy forces without any realistic counter-measures. (USAF)

7   The Vietnamese Lunar New Year, or Tet holiday, is an important celebration in Vietnamese culture.

ARVN 3d Division commander Brigadier-General Vu Van Giai enjoys a moment with Marine advisors in I Corps prior to the Easter Offensive. The good times did not last past this Marine Corps birthday event. (Author's collection)

existed. Abrams directed that likely avenues of approach and assembly areas be pre-planned for B-52 Arc Light strikes.

By January 1972, the 3d ARVN Division was responsible for everything north of Highway 9, including all Fire Support bases and combat outposts. Division commander Brigadier-General Vu Van Giai visited his ARVN units and the Marines in the field daily. His command had the many problems of a new one: the soldiers were a mix of varied quality, untrained as a unit, and equipped from existing Vietnamese sources. A USMACV advisor felt: "We were getting college students who had evaded the draft for long periods, also interpreters who had worked for US forces." These were "city slickers" and not the average ARVN soldier from a rural background. This had a definite effect on morale and training in their ability to hold I Corps' "Ring of Steel." One result was that Brigadier-General Vu Van Giai dismissed suggestions for offensive action to the west until the division was in a better position to accomplish this.

On January 27, 1972, a USAF gunship was shot down by an SA-2 surface-to-air missile at 5,000ft over Khe Sanh while patrolling over Route 9, an abnormal anti-aircraft hazard for the region. Other outposts reported stand-off attacks by mortars and rockets, as well as ground vehicle movements made at night. As the situation developed, reports of offensive actions were perceived through February 1972. By March 5, 1972, a South Vietnamese operation began east of Hue City, running into North Vietnamese units. Rather than considering this a challenge to MR 1, it was seen by the intelligence community as a threat to MR 2. This was the view held by MR 1's Lieutenant-General Hoang Xuan Lam and his American counterpart Major-General Kroesen, as well as USMACV and the American Embassy. Of interest was the apparent lack of concern for any direct attack across the DMZ or the use of mechanized units, despite the fact that the majority of the South Vietnamese positions were within artillery or rocket range.

Two fresh NVA units introduced in MR 1 were the NVA 202d and 203d Armored regiments, and vehicles with the infantry divisions. The North Vietnamese had armored units and previously used them for some time in the south. Recent experience was available in 1971 from the NVA use of armor during the *Lam Son 719* incursion and in their attacks on the Plain of Jars in Laos. A variety of armored vehicles were encountered, differing in nomenclature and technical details. There was a mix of Soviet- and Chinese-manufactured equipment, for example the Soviet T-54/55 or the Chinese Type 59 main battle tanks; the Soviet PT-76 amphibious tank or the similar Chinese Type 63; and the Soviet BTR-50 or Chinese Type 63 armored personnel carriers. This variety was also witnessed in artillery and anti-aircraft weapons.

THE CAMPAIGN

THE SPRING OFFENSIVE

Vietnamization was battle tested on March 30, 1972 when the North Vietnamese began conventional attacks coinciding with the withdrawal of American forces from the region.[8] By then, US troop levels were at 69,000, with 11 maneuver battalions, three artillery battalions in country, and no fighter squadrons. The communists invaded with an initial wave of six divisions—an effort that struck toward Quang Tri and Hue cities in MR 1, Kontum and Pleiku in MR 2, and An Loc and Saigon in MR 3. Whether these were to be simultaneous or consecutive attacks is now hard to determine (they actually began in the north on March 30, 1972, in the south on April 4, 1972, and in the central area on April 11, 1972). The NVA relied on bad weather and combined arms to defeat the South Vietnamese, which they believed lacked effective American assistance. The magnitude of the attack was such that ultimately up to 12 NVA divisions entered South Vietnam on these three fronts.

The USMACV FRAC in MR 1 reported that three divisions, five separate infantry regiments, seven sapper battalions, three or more artillery regiments, and two armored regiments were in the Quang Tri Province attacks. Defensive positions across the DMZ were overwhelmed by intense North Vietnamese artillery fire, followed up by determined infantry attacks that the South Vietnamese could not cope with. The American response was to counter with air and naval strikes along the DMZ in South Vietnam and then into North Vietnam. These were met by sophisticated anti-aircraft and coastal defenses.

The ARVN 3d Division was caught off balance in the process of rotating forces among the positions south of the DMZ. The Division Artillery Group was at Camp Carroll with 105mm to 175mm guns in 26 pieces. The ARVN 56th Regiment was in the process of replacing the ARVN 2d

Lacking air and naval support of its own, the NVA made extensive use of anti-aircraft artillery and missiles to counter Allied airpower. Most Allied aircraft losses were due to low-altitude weapons systems. (PAVN)

8   The Paris Peace Talks were suspended at the request of the American delegation on March 23, 1972, to be resumed only if the North Vietnamese would engage in discussions on specific topics.

Initial deployment of North and South Vietnamese forces, March 30–April 1, 1972

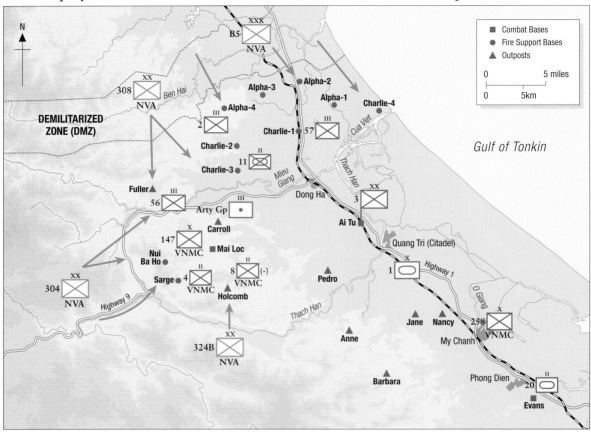

The untried and recently organized ARVN 3d Division was caught off guard and collapsed under concentrated attack by a better-organized force on the ground. One regiment and artillery group surrendered, two regiments were defeated, and the supporting Marines pushed back by heavy infantry, artillery, and armored attacks.

Regiment at Camp Carroll, Khe Gio, and FSB Fuller. The 2d Regiment was to occupy outposts Alpha-4, Charlie-2, and Charlie-3. The ARVN 57th Regiment covered the remainder of the front from Dong Ha, north to the DMZ, including Alpha-1, Alpha-2, and Alpha-3. The Marines from VNMC Brigade 147 were at Nui Ba Ho, Sarge, and FSB Holcomb. VNMC Brigade 258 was further to the south at FSBs Nancy and Barbara. The direction and impact of the NVA assault disrupted any coherent response. The arrival of North Vietnamese armor on the battlefield after the artillery and infantry attacks gave way to an outbreak of "tank fever" among the confused South Vietnamese. Brigadier-General Vu Van Giai found himself trying to stem the civilian and military disorder over the Dong Ha Bridge, demanding: "Show me a tank and I will go with you and we will destroy it together!" A critical point in the initial fight was now in the making on the northern front.

From March 30 to April 4, 1972, the 3d Division suffered the destruction and surrender of its 56th Regiment and Division Artillery Group while conducting harrowing withdrawals of the 57th Regiment and Marine Brigade 147. Eight South Vietnamese Fire Support bases or outposts were lost before the communists came to pause in MR 1 to refuel and refit, as strong attacks continued in MRs 2 and 3.[9] Marine Brigade 258 and the

9   From April 5 to 7, 1972, the communists captured Loc Ninh in MR 3 and An Loc was surrounded; the American air and naval bombardment of North Vietnam resumed on April 7 as well.

NAVY CROSS CITATION: RAY L. SMITH

Ray L. Smith was recognized for actions as a captain from March 30 through April 1, 1972. He was a native of Oklahoma. Entering the USMC in 1965, he retired a major-general in 1999. At the time considered, he was located at an outpost with the 4th Marine Battalion. Attacked by some two battalions of NVA regulars, under heavy artillery fire, he repeatedly exposed himself to danger to control friendly air support. With the weather conditions precluding this effort, he led a group of Marines to break out of the exposed position. In the course of this, he threw his body on barbed wire and booby traps to allow 28 Marines to escape. With him in the lead, although injured, they regained friendly lines. His citation read:

> For extraordinary heroism during the period 30 March to 1 April 1972 while serving as advisory to a Vietnamese command group numbering approximately 250 Vietnamese Marines located on a small hilltop outpost in the Republic of Vietnam. With the command group repulsing several savage enemy assaults, and subjected to a continuing hail of fire from an attacking force estimated to be of two-battalion strength, Captain Smith repeatedly exposed himself to heavy fire while directing friendly air support. When adverse weather conditions precluded further close air support, he attempted to lead the group, now reduced to only 28 Vietnamese Marines, to the safety of friendly lines. An enemy soldier opened fire upon the Marines at the precise moment that they had balked when encountering an outer defense ring of barbed wire. Captain Smith returned accurate fire, disposing of the attacker, and then threw himself backwards on top of the booby-trap-infested wire barrier. Swiftly, the remaining Marines moved over the crushed wire, stepping on Captain Smith's prostrate body, until all had passed safely through the barrier. Although suffering severe cuts and bruises, Captain Smith succeeded in leading the Marines to the safety of friendly lines. His great personal valor and unrelenting devotion to duty reflected the highest credit on himself, the Marine Corps, and the United States Naval Service.

ARVN 1st Armored Brigade barely held at Dong Ha as Brigadier-General Vu Van Giai regrouped his division south of the Cua Viet River during the first week of April. With a forward command post at the Ai Tu Combat Base, Vu Van Giai's main headquarters stayed at the Quang Tri City Citadel, along with MACV Advisory Team 155. Vietnamese Marine Division G-3 operations and Assistant Senior Marine Advisor Lieutenant-Colonel Gerald H. Turley stated that "the main North Vietnamese thrust was halted and the communist army's time schedule for seizing Quang Tri City within seven days was disrupted."

North Vietnamese Army supporting arms included armor and artillery, such as this T-54/55 tank in Quang Tri Province in 1972. (PAVN)

EASTER SUNDAY AT DONG HA

Sunday, April 2, 1972 proved to be a fateful day for the ARVN 3d Division defending northern Quang Tri Province along the DMZ. After three days of continuous artillery fire and coordinated infantry assaults, it appeared the North Vietnamese were making their main attack along the axis of the national highway (*Quoc Lo, QL*) 1. At this time Camp Carroll and Mai Loc bases to the west were still barely in South Vietnamese hands, as resistance to the north of the Cam Lo River crumbled. The NVA 308th Division's thrust south from the DMZ gained momentum as each 3d

The defense of Dong Ha, April 2–4, 1972

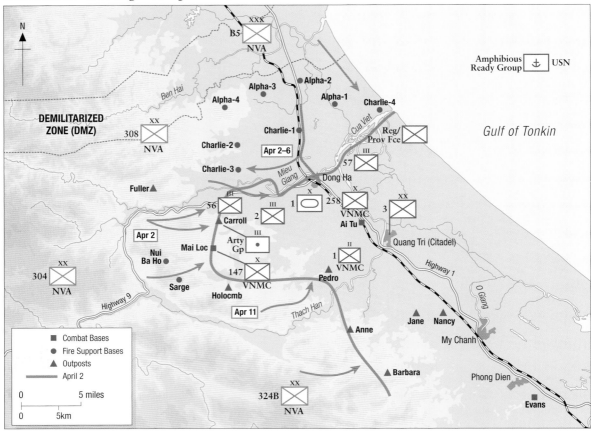

Dong Ha river crossings became the focus of South Vietnamese defense and North Vietnamese attacks in the first days. Armor and Marines held despite losses while counter-actions were being organized, including extensive American air and naval gunfire fire support. The possibility of employing American ground forces existed, but were not required to blunt the attack.

Division outpost and fire support base fell. Intelligence reports estimated that three NVA mechanized divisions were attacking with approximately 10,000 infantry, 150 T-54 and PT-76 tanks, 75 tracked anti-aircraft vehicles, an artillery regiment with 47 122mm or 130mm guns, and anti-aircraft missile units.

By midday Easter Sunday, nothing was on the Highway 1 axis between the enemy and the coveted Quang Tri City except a river, a bridge, a battalion of Vietnamese Marines, and M48 tanks. On the ground with them in MR 1 were the American advisors. The VNMC 3d Battalion, with Captain John W. Ripley as its sole advisor, was spread along Highway 9 from Cam Lo to Dong Ha. Ripley was on his second tour in Vietnam, with background as a US Naval Academy graduate and in US Marine Force Recon and British Royal Marine assignments. He provided "advice" and fire support coordination to the 700-man unit on the south side of the Cua Viet River to gain enough time for the ARVN 3d Division to organize a new line of defense south of the Thach Han River.

With a report of approaching tanks at 1000hrs, Major Le Ba Binh, the 3d Battalion commander, was ordered by his brigade to defend Dong Ha, and to "hold at all costs." The brigade commander sent four jeep-mounted 106mm recoilless rifles north for support to hold the first river obstacle between Dong Ha and Ai Tu, the division forward command post. Also sent forward were 42 brand-new M48 main battle tanks of Lieutenant-Colonel Nguyen Huu Ly's ARVN 20th Tank Squadron/Battalion. Ripley now expected the worst: a column of communist PT-76 and T-54 tanks were approaching, military and civilian refugees were clogging the roads out of Dong Ha, and no further units were available to help.

A large red and yellow North Vietnamese flag was seen flying over the railway bridge and NVA infantry were moving across it and the highway bridge as the Marine infantry and ARVN armor arrived. Ripley recalled an "absolute firestorm" of communist artillery fire hitting Dong Ha at this point. Enemy tanks appeared on the horizon to the north, sending up "rooster tails" of dust as they barreled down Highway 1. Naval gunfire from US Navy destroyers in the Gulf of Tonkin had some effect. Oily columns of black smoke rose over the north bank of the river as air strikes by South Vietnamese A-1 Skyraiders hit the communist armored column backed up to the north of the bridge. But this was not enough to halt them.

At 1200hrs, the South Vietnamese M48s began firing at the North Vietnamese tank column, knocking out six vehicles. At about 1215hrs, while the first NVA tank nosed onto the north side of the highway bridge, Vietnamese Marine Sergeant Huyn Van Luom, a veteran of many years fighting, took two M72 light anti-tank assault weapons and walked up to the south side of the bridge. Although he was a section leader, he moved forward alone. As he reached the bridge, he positioned two ammunition boxes filled with dirt and placed a single roll of concertina wire in front of him. Luom coolly extended both rocket launchers as the NVA tank started across the bridge.

It was a ludicrous situation, the 90 lb Marine crouched in the firing position to engage a 36-ton behemoth bearing down on the meager fortification. The tank jerked to a halt; perhaps the tank commander could not believe his eyes, as the lone Marine took aim. Luom fired; the round went high and to the right. The tank started to ease forward again as Luom picked up the second rocket, aimed, and fired. This round ricocheted off the bow plate, detonating on the turret ring, jamming the turret. The communist tank commander backed off the bridge into cover, making the worst decision he could have. All at once, the Marines along the river saw that enemy armor could be stopped. The whole incident only took a few minutes. Sergeant Luom grinned and the whole front breathed easier. Captain Ripley gave him credit for "singlehandedly stopping the momentum of the entire enemy attack."

At 1245hrs, the 3d Division command post radioed the US Army advisor with the ARVN 20th Tank Battalion, Major James E. Smock. Authorization was given to demolish the Dong Ha Bridge immediately. Higher headquarters had been informed of the decision, and, if necessary, additional explosives would be sent. Major Smock, on an ARVN tank, passed Ripley and called,

Combat action at Dong Ha with VNMC infantry and ARVN armor. Their fierce resistance stalled the communist offensive at this point and time. Major J.E. Smock is in the center and Captain J.W. Ripley on the right. (© David Burnett/ Contact Press Images)

Battalion command post for the 3d Marine Battalion at Dong Ha, April 1972. Major Le Ba Binh is on the radio at the map, with Captain J.W. Ripley on the left. Sometimes described as a back-pocket effort, the American advisor was the link to American firepower. (© David Burnett/Contact Press Images)

"Hey Marine, climb aboard and let's go blow a bridge." With his US Army Ranger and Royal Marine demolition expertise, when Ripley heard this he replied that he had "always wanted to blow a bridge." The two Americans, with a couple of M48 tanks, moved forward to within 100 yards of the bridge. Still hull down, the tanks stopped at this point and Ripley and Smock dismounted, shielded from the enemy view by a French-era bunker. From the bunker to the bridge was open space swept by enemy small-arms and mortar fire. The Vietnamese Marines in forward positions fired at the north bank as the two advisors came up. The sun was bright and the weather had cleared, but there were no aircraft overhead or naval gunfire coming in.

The two men ran across the open space to the approach to the bridge. There they found ARVN combat engineers hastily stacking 500 lb of TNT and C4 plastic explosives at the juncture of the bridge and the approach ramp. Ripley, quickly surveying the situation, realized that in such a location upon detonation, the bridge would simply "flap" in place and not drop as intended. After a quick conference with Smock, it was agreed that the explosives should be placed along the girders under the bridge. As a chain-link fence topped by barbed wire prevented access to the underpinnings of the bridge, Ripley would have to clear the fence, while Smock would then lift the explosives over it, after which Ripley would place the boxes underneath the span.

With effort, Ripley succeeded in making his way up into the steel channels of the bridge. Crawling back and forth between the beams, he placed the explosives in staggered alignment between the five channels created by the six beams. Smock muscled the 50 lb ammunition crates to within Ripley's reach after climbing the fence with each crate. Smock insisted there was enough power to blow the bridge and "three others like it." Ripley assured Smock, "You tankers don't know anything." All the time they were watched and fired at by the NVA from the opposite bank 50 yards away. Both were exhausted by the effort and paused for a rest and a smoke before proceeding with a final task: the fusing of the charges with both electric and conventional blasting caps.

Not finding the Vietnamese engineers or blasting machine, Ripley tried to set the charges off with the battery of a wrecked jeep. When this did not work, the fate of the northern provinces rested on 30 minutes of sputtering time fuse working its way to ten crates of high-explosives. Smock and Ripley "waited and hoped" as the telltale smoking time fuse neared its end. Suddenly, the bridge blew. The chosen span, curling in the predicted twisting manner, was severed from the pilings and settled into the river. The smoking open space between the north and south banks was a beautiful sight. At 1630hrs, Ripley reported to the division command post that the Dong Ha Bridge was destroyed and that Major Smock had damaged the railroad bridge upstream.

All firing stopped and there was calm for a few moments, then on the north side noise was evident once more as NVA tanks shifted their positions for PT-76 amphibious tanks to come forward to the river's edge. The enemy was still determined to cross and Ripley rapidly called for a naval gunfire mission. The destroyer gunfire support ship fired a salvo that caught four tanks on the riverbank. Subsequently, A-1 Skyraiders and a B-52 Stratofortress bombing strike, scheduled for the area, silenced the remaining armor activity to the north and east of Dong Ha. Later, this critical support was disrupted when an American RB-66 electronic warfare aircraft (call sign BAT-21) was hit by a surface-to-air-missile and Seventh Air Force and USMACV took fire support coordination out of the hands of the local commanders in order to recover the aircrews. After 11 days, with several helicopters and crews being lost, a single survivor was recovered.

With their armored thrusts thwarted at Dong Ha and the Cua Viet, the determined North Vietnamese exerted pressure elsewhere, capturing Mai Loc and Camp Carroll. The Cam Lo Bridge to the west was the only available crossing point, and the NVA effort shifted in that direction. More naval gunfire and air strikes were called for, and again squelched enemy movement as all night long hundreds of projectiles were directed at the enemy. The battle for Dong Ha was still in doubt, but there was no question the communist armored assault was halted by the efforts of "a few good men" on Easter Sunday. For their actions that day, Captain Ripley was awarded the Navy Cross and Major Smock the Silver Star Medal—America's second- and third-highest awards for courage. But Ripley still recalled Sergeant Luom's action in stopping the first tank at the bridge as the "bravest single act of heroism I've ever heard of, witnessed, or experienced."

An air photograph of the bridges at Dong Ha recorded destruction of these vital crossings. Note the cratered indications of an air strike as well. Ripley's highway bridge is to the right, Smock's railway bridge is on the left. (Author's collection)

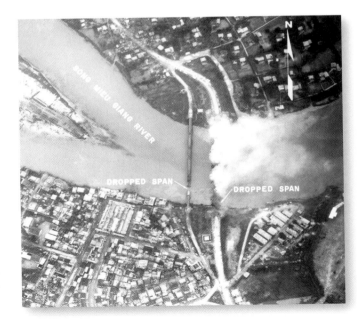

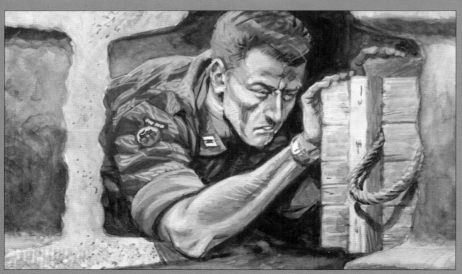

THE DONG HA BRIDGE, APRIL 2, 1972 (PP. 44–45)

The 500ft-long, two-lane Dong Ha highway bridge was constructed by the Americans to handle the heavy military traffic across the Cua Viet River. Existing pilings were reinforced with steel beams across which a wooden roadway was laid, but without much concern for foot traffic or pedestrian railings.

(**1**) At 1215hrs on Easter Sunday, the first NVA tank appeared on the north side of the highway bridge. VNMC Sergeant Huyn Van Luom (**1a**) moved forward alone onto the bridge with an M72 LAW (**1b**). The M72 Anti-Tank Rocket or Light Anti-Armor Weapon (LAW or LAAW) was a self-contained system that delivered a 66mm high-explosive anti-tank rocket to a distance of 1,000m (200m was the realistic range). A shaped charge missile could penetrate the armor of most vehicles of the time. It was the standard individual weapon for assault men but required nerve to use on the battlefield under fire.

Luom fired at the NVA tank as it started to cross toward him. His first round missed, but the second ricocheted off the bow plate, detonated on the turret ring, and jammed the M48's turret. Luom's brave action resulted in the tank backing off the bridge into cover: singlehandedly, he had stopped the momentum of the entire NVA attack.

At 1245hrs that same day, authorization was given to demolish the Dong Ha Bridge immediately. Major James E. Smock (the US Army advisor with the ARVN 20th Tank Battalion) and Captain John W. Ripley (sole advisor to the VNMC 3d Battalion) moved forward to the bridge under fire. Ripley cleared the chain-link fence topped by barbed wire preventing access to the underpinnings of the bridge (**2**), and then Smock lifted the explosives over the fence to Ripley.

With effort, Ripley succeeded in making his way up into the steel channels of the bridge (**3**). Crawling back and forth between the beams, he placed the explosives in staggered alignment between the five channels created by the six beams. All the time both Ripley and Smock were watched and fired at by the NVA from the opposite bank 50 yards away.

With the channels filled, Ripley rapidly made his way back to the bank (**4**), where after pausing to recover, the final act of fusing the charges with both electric and conventional blasting caps was done. They were forced to use a sputtering time fuse to ignite the high-explosives. Eventually, just before 1630hrs, the bridge blew, and the span settled into the river.

NAVY CROSS CITATION: JOHN W. RIPLEY

John W. Ripley, a native of West Virginia, was educated at the US Naval Academy. Entering the USMC in 1957, he retired a colonel in 1992. Ripley was recognized for actions as a captain on April 2 (Easter Sunday), 1972, when his unit, the 3d Marine Battalion, was placed in the defense of Dong Ha, including the critical bridge. His citation read:

> For extraordinary heroism on 2 April 1972 while serving as the Senior Marine Advisor to the 3d VNMC Infantry Battalion in the Republic of Vietnam. Upon receipt of a report that a rapidly moving, mechanized, North Vietnamese army force, estimated at a reinforced divisional strength, was attacking south along Route 1, the 3d Vietnamese Marine Corps Infantry Battalion was positioned to defend a key village in the surrounding area. It became imperative that a vital bridge be destroyed if the overall security of the northern provinces of Military Region 1 was to be maintained.

Advancing to the bridge to personally supervise this most dangerous but vitally important assignment, Captain Ripley located a large amount of explosives which had been prepositioned there earlier, access to which was blocked by a chain-link fence. In order to reposition the approximately 500 pounds of explosive, Captain Ripley was obliged to reach up and hand-walk along the beams while his body dangled beneath the bridge. On five separate occasions, in the face of constant enemy fire, he moved to points along the bridge and with the aid of another advisor who pushed the explosives to him, securely emplaced them. He detonated the charges and destroyed the bridge, thereby stopping the enemy assault. By his heroic actions and extraordinary courage, Captain Ripley undoubtedly was instrumental in saving an untold number of lives. His inspiring efforts reflected great credit upon himself, the Marine Corps, and the United States Naval Service.

On April 3, 1972, the Vietnamese Joint General Staff sent the entire Vietnamese Marine Division to MR 1, but Lieutenant-General Le Nguyen Khang was ordered to place his brigades under the direct control of Lieutenant-General Hoang Xuan Lam's I Corps. While the 3d Division held Dong Ha from attacks across the DMZ to the north, the emphasis of the battle shifted significantly to the western approaches of the Ai Tu Combat Base and Quang Tri City. From April 9 to 11, the battle swung in the balance around FSB Pedro, with substantial artillery and armored duels. Lieutenant-Colonel Turley reported, "The invading North Vietnamese divisions continued to press their attacks toward Quang Tri City with enemy armor and infantry forces using the Cam Lo Bridge as their primary crossing point. Once south of the Cam Lo–Cua Viet River, NVA units moved on Dong Ha

Naval gunfire was a force multiplier for the Allied forces, as seen by the cruiser USS *Newport News* employed here. (USN)

American and Vietnamese Marines with a TOW missile launcher that provided a degree of anti-armor direct support on the battlefield. Major P.E. Carlson is on the left, and 9th Marine Battalion commander Lieutenant-Colonel Nguyen Kim De on the right. TOWs did not arrive in numbers until later in May 1972. (USMC)

from the west. Other enemy forces moved south, passing FSB Carroll and Mai Loc, on toward Route 557 and FSB Pedro." There, enemy tank–infantry assaults were repulsed by defending Vietnamese Marines, and NVA dead and destroyed vehicles were left on the battlefield. Attempts by the I Corps commander Hoang Xuan Lam to conduct a counter-offensive from April 14 to 23 (Operation *Quang Trung 729*) failed to get off the ground despite heavy American air support, including strategic bomber Arc Light strikes. The slow rate of advance only seemed to focus increased NVA attention on the westward approaches to Quang Tri and Hue cities.[10]

The demands on the ARVN 3d Division command and control system, which had been reinforced with as many as 36 battalion-size units, increased. Major-General Kroesen pointed out that at no time were the 3d Division's logistics resources expanded and that communication links continued to be maintained with outside commands to ensure needed support. South Vietnamese losses were estimated by USMACV at 63 guns or howitzers (155mm and 105mm), 37 tanks, and 89 armored personnel carriers—a total of more than 240 vehicles of all kinds. Personnel losses through death, injury, or desertion could only be estimated (Vietnamese Marines lost some 1,808 killed or wounded through the month of April). Colonel Donald J. Metcalf, the senior US Army advisor to Brigadier-General Vu Van Giai, believed this arrangement created the situation that did not carry "the allegiance and loyalty" necessary to conduct successful combat operations. Despite these difficulties, Lam refused to use the two division-level headquarters placed at his command by the Joint General Staff, the Vietnamese Marine Division, and the ARVN Ranger Command. Major-General Kroesen wrote that Lam dismissed suggestions to provide a multi-division structure to fight the battle north of the Hai Van Pass as "unnecessary and impractical." The chief of the general staff, General Cao Van Vien, recalled these commands were "never utilized or given a mission."

Lieutenant-General Hoang Xuan Lam's focus on a premature counter-offensive prevented him and his staff from even considering the obvious problems of defending Quang Tri or Hue cities. The contentious command issues of *Lam Son 719* were again felt when Lam and Khang refused to deal directly with each other. As a result, Major-General Kroesen and Colonel Joshua W. Dorsey III, the senior Marine advisor to Lieutenant-General Le Nguyen Khang, served as the only means of contact between the two Vietnamese generals. According to the Marine Division G-3 advisor,

10 Bombing of Hanoi and Haiphong were resumed on April 15, 1972, with restrictions being lifted on most targets. A wave of protests took place in the United States as a result of the increased fighting.

Lieutenant-General Khang and his staff monitored every tactical move as they waited impatiently to assume control of all three of the Marine brigades.

For Major-General Kroesen, a sign of the lack of effective authority within I Corps was the participation of the Marine Division and Ranger Command in issuing guidance, responding to complaints and questions, and providing "unsought advice and counsel concerning their forces to anyone who would listen." Lieutenant-General Hoang Xuan Lam compounded this by going directly to 3d Division units—particularly the ARVN 1st Armored Brigade, whose advisor, US Army Lieutenant-Colonel Louis C. Wagner, Jr., complained about receiving orders from the corps commander, the corps commander's deputy, and his operations officer. Major-General Kroesen concluded all this undercut the authority of Brigadier-General Vu Van Giai by planting the seeds of distrust and disobedience that would culminate with near mutiny at the end of April 1972.

Effective tactical air support was provided to Free World forces from Seventh Fleet aircraft carriers on Yankee Station. (USN)

At this stage, by April 24, the 3d Division was organized around five mixed task forces.[11] The ARVN 1st Armored Brigade along with the 57th Regiment held the area from Highway 1 to 5km east, bounded by the Cam Lo River in the north and the Ai Tu Combat Base in the south. Marine Brigade 147 was at the Ai Tu Combat Base with the division forward command post, conducting defensive operations in an arc to the west. The 2d Regiment defended the area southwest of Ai Tu to the Thach Han River. The 1st Ranger Group was located south of the Thach Han River, Marine Brigade 369 was farther south near Hai Lang on FSBs Nancy and Jane, and Marine Brigade 258 was refitting at Hue. Major-General Kroesen described a pattern of inaction established within the 3d Division's area where "no orders, threats, or exhortations" were able to force subordinates to move or stay if they disagreed. Both generals Hoang Xuan Lam and Vu Van Giai were losing control on the battlefield to this general state of confused inertia, as each appeared willing to let American airpower win the fight for them. With this, the NVA moved to cut off Dong Ha and Quang Tri City in order to cause the collapse of the South Vietnamese defenders.

CONFUSION AT QUANG TRI CITY

On April 27, 1972, the North Vietnamese renewed their general offensive throughout the Quang Tri Front. The NVA 308th Division attacked Dong Ha, "liberating" it on the afternoon of April 28. Communist forces pushed the defenders back toward Highway 1 and south toward Quang Tri City

11 Dak To in MR 2 was captured on April 23, 1972.

The defense of Quang Tri City, April 22–29, 1972

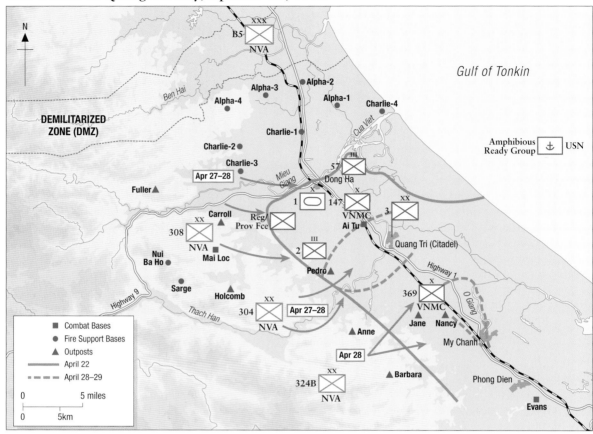

With delay to rearm and regroup, NVA forces moved on the key headquarters at Quang Tri City. The South Vietnamese forces were unable to create a cohesive defense to counter the subsequent assault by artillery and armor, despite American supporting arms. The loss of the provincial capital was the result.

using 122mm and 130mm artillery, T-54/55 main battle tanks, and infantry. The NVA 304th Division attacked toward the Ai Tu Combat Base. At the same time, the NVA 324th Division struck further to the south. As a result, Highway 1 was blocked and Quang Tri City was cut off from the rest of I Corps. This situation was compounded as NVA artillery hit the Ai Tu ammunition dump and stocks went up in blazes. On April 29, Brigadier-General Vu Van Giai issued orders for a general withdrawal to positions along the O'Khe and My Chanh rivers but was then overruled by Lieutenant-General Hoang Xuan Lam. The various accounts of events for the actions that followed merged intent with action, so Vu Van Giai and Hoang Xuan Lam's command dynamics are difficult to recreate. General Cao Van Vien commented that the Quang Tri debacle involved some intricacies "that only the principals could clarify."

Early Sunday morning, on April 30, 1972, a regimental-size NVA force supported by armor was assembled southwest of Ai Tu. Up to this point, Lieutenant-Colonel Nguyen Nang Bao's Marine Brigade 147, with brigade advisor Major Jim R. Joy, had been able to use artillery and tank support to halt the North Vietnamese attacks. But then ammunition supplies ran low, and the battalion-size 20th Tank Squadron was being parceled out south of the Thach Han River in an effort to keep Highway 1 open. American naval gunfire could not be used effectively against the enemy staging area, because it was at a maximum effective range. The Marines called in aircraft with attack sorties striking close to the front lines. But even heavy air attacks could not save the untenable salient that had developed north of the Thach Han River. Upon seeing the supporting tanks moving to the south, the remaining ARVN infantry drifted away from their positions, as all types of vehicles began running out of fuel and rumors were rampant. Colonel Metcalf recalled several thousand troops and hundreds of vehicles bunched up on Highway 1 with no escape route except into withering fire and panic. At this stage, according to Metcalf, the higher headquarters for I Corps, South Vietnamese Marines, and Rangers all added to the confusion by passing contrary orders, which Brigadier-General Vu Van Giai and his staff were unable to sort out.

VNMC Brigade 147 commander Lieutenant-Colonel Nguyen Nang Bao. From North Vietnam, he was a 19-year veteran and graduate of Marine Corps schools. (USMC)

A critical move occurred with the decision to pull Marine Brigade 369 out of FSB Jane to reopen Highway 1, which exposed the 3d Division's whole southern flank. At daybreak on April 30, 1972, Colonel Pham Van Chung of Marine Brigade 369, with brigade senior advisor Major Robert F. Sheridan, sent a battalion north on Highway 1 in an attempt to break through to Quang Tri City on orders from the division and corps. The battalion met heavy automatic weapon and recoilless rifle fire along the way and waited for these enemy positions to be hit by tactical air strikes. The Marine battalion then reached a bottleneck between the O'Khe River Bridge and Hai Lang, where the communists were positioned along the highway. With the destruction of this enemy force, the exodus of fugitives fleeing south came pouring down the road, and the prospect of the battalion linking up with the units in Quang Tri City faded. The Marine battalion was low on ammunition, overextended, and unable to move up the road through the flow of refugees. Colonel Pham Van Chung directed the battalion to return to the O'Khe River Bridge and hold it for the units breaking out from the north.

The best chance of holding Quang Tri City at this moment seemed to be Marine Brigade 147, the only tactical unit remaining in any cohesive condition to fight. Metcalf called it "our last ditch defense." At noon on April 30, 1972, Brigadier-General Vu Van Giai ordered Brigade 147 from the Ai Tu Combat Base into the city proper. The remaining 3d Division units could then form a defensive line south of the Thach Han River, while the following 1st Armored Brigade tanks and armored personnel carriers would be used to keep Highway 1 open toward Hue. Lieutenant-General Hoang Xuan Lam was notified of this plan and acknowledged it, but no specific approval was provided, and no orders were issued by I Corps.

Marine infantry at Quang Tri Province, South Vietnam, in 1972. They were the tip of the spear in battlefield victory or defeat. Though fighting on foot, they could arrive in battle by air, land, or sea. (USMC)

Lieutenant-Colonel Nguyen Nang Bao and Major Joy were briefed by the 3d Division staff, and the plan began smoothly enough as the brigade headquarters and artillery battalion departed Ai Tu. The Marine advisors effectively directed and controlled tactical air strikes, artillery, and naval gunfire missions, slowing the communist forces' pursuit and permitting the brigade's orderly and covered withdrawal. This went well until the column reached the approach to Quang Tri City and found division engineers had already destroyed the bridges across the Thach Han River. The Marine infantry waded and swam across the river at the bridge site and moved directly into their fighting positions. The brigade artillery tried to tow its howitzers across a ford, but the swift current and soft bottom of the river mired the effort. Lost in the attempt were 18 howitzers and 22 vehicles. The armored brigade fared worse than the Marine brigade when its recently assigned commander had to destroy 12 tanks, 18 howitzers, and numerous armored personnel carriers for lack of fuel and ammunition. Fortunately, the 20th Tank Squadron forded the river north of the bridges with 16 of its remaining M48 battle tanks. By nightfall, Brigade 147 and remnant forces occupied the defenses that were planned to hold Quang Tri City.

Advisors and Vietnamese Marines in Quang Tri Province. Living conditions were shared even if sparse, as it was a "grass roots" existence not for the weak or soft. (*Leatherneck* magazine)

COLLAPSE

On the morning of May 1, 1972, Lieutenant-General Hoang Xuan Lam informed Brigadier-General Vu Van Giai that all Quang Tri positions were to be held and no withdrawal of any kind was authorized. This directive was from Saigon, with Lam receiving his orders from President Nguyen Van Thieu. But signals intelligence arrived that indicated the city would be hit again that evening by a heavy artillery attack estimated at 10,000 rounds of munitions. With this, Vu Van Giai decided that any further defense of Quang Tri City would be fruitless. "To protect the lives of all of you," Vu Van Giai authorized units to fall back farther south; at this time, he was in no position to stop them. Giai and Colonel Metcalf were in conflict, with Metcalf insisting that Vietnamese Marines could hold the Citadel "indefinitely" with American supporting arms. This had been his advice the previous month when Marine Brigade 258 was left to cover the division's withdrawal through Dong Ha.

VNMC Brigade 258 commander Lieutenant-Colonel Ngo Van Dinh. He was an 18-year veteran and graduate of Marine Corps schools. (USMC)

At 1215hrs on May 1, 1972, the chief of staff of the 3d Division walked into MACV Advisory Team 155's bunker and, using the American radio circuits, called all subordinate commanders: "Brigadier-General Giai has released all commanders to fight their way to the My Chanh River!" Within 30 minutes, I Corps commander Lieutenant-General Hoang Xuan Lam again sent "stand and die" orders. At this point, all of Vu Van Giai's subordinate senior commanders refused to obey, stating Giai could withdraw with them or be left behind—a threat that, according to Major-General Kroesen, they proceeded to carry out. Other units did not respond to the change, or refused to deviate from their original orders to pull back. Colonel Metcalf was left to watch his counterparts on the division staff pack their belongings totally unaware and unconcerned by the situation. Shortly afterward, Colonel Metcalf radioed Marine Brigade 147 and said, "The ARVN are pulling out; advisors may stay with their units or join me [for evacuation by helicopter]." Major Jim Joy responded that the Brigade 147 advisors would stay with their units. Although the offshore US Navy and Marine Amphibious Ready Group (formerly the Special Landing Force) was alerted, the pickup was accomplished by USAF Sikorsky CH-54 Jolly Green Giant search and rescue helicopters.

Recalling the division's previous desertion of his brigade at Mai Loc, Lieutenant-Colonel Nguyen Nang Bao refused to defend what all others were now abandoning. The sight of the 3d Division soldiers departing with their families did nothing to engender the desire for a last stand. Luckily for the Marines, their dependents were in MR 3, unlike most ARVN units whose soldiers fought and lived in the same locale. The presence and safety of family members was a constant drain on manpower and the commander's

HIGHWAY OF HORROR, MAY 1, 1972 (PP. 54–55)

As Quang Tri Province fell into NVA hands, there was only one major exit route out for those wishing to escape: Highway (QL) 1. This scene shows the confusion and panic occurring along the highway on May 1, south of Quang Tri City.

The column of thousands of civilian refugees (**1**) and ARVN military (**2**) heading south was hit by communist artillery, support weapons, and small-arms fire from NVA troops dug in on the roadside, and were trapped on the highway as it became blocked in several places. Coherent military movement of South Vietnamese forces was prevented by this incident, as well as lack of fuel and ammunition. It should be recognized that the ARVN division members had families in their operational area. Here, we see an NVA shell or mortar round exploding among the crowded civilians (**3**), causing loss of life.

The variety of bicycles, cyclos, omnibuses, military trucks, and armored vehicles (**4**) impeded by pedestrians and luggage clogged the road, with little alternative except to head out cross-country in low-lying terrain blocked by waterways, hoping to avoid NVA fire. Many military vehicles and artillery pieces were abandoned, and civilian families separated in the confusion. It was a disaster for both troops and civilians caught up in the event. Were the communists merely blocking a military withdrawal on the Highway of Horror, or deliberately killing civilians as they headed south on Highway 1? The full horror of the attack on Highway 1 only became known a few months later.

attention. A little after 1430hrs, the brigade headquarters was southwest of the Citadel, where the unit expected to be joined by Brigadier-General Vu Van Giai and his staff before pushing on to the south to link up with Marine Brigade 369 at My Chanh. The move had been coordinated earlier by Major Joy and Colonel Metcalf. In the confusion, the division commander and staff did not arrive. Metcalf stated Giai left him and the other advisors at the Citadel, while Kroesen stated the Marines had left Giai, with Bao holding the bag for both. Colonel Metcalf then radioed Major Joy to inform him that the linkup would not be made and that the American advisors should resort to their own devices as it was every man for himself. In what was taken as pro forma, Colonel Metcalf reiterated that the Marine advisors could join him for the helicopter evacuation from Quang Tri City. Major Joy again declined, and the departing Advisory Team 155 senior advisor responded with, "Good luck!" At 1635hrs, Brigade 147 moved east toward the coast and then turned south. After making several difficult stream crossings, the column arrived in the vicinity of Hai Lang, 6 miles south of Quang Tri City.

VNMC Brigade 369 commander Colonel Pham Van Chung. From North Vietnam, he was the senior-ranking brigade commander, and graduate of Marine Corps schools. (USMC)

The intermingled civilian and military stragglers prevented movement on the highway, and the cross-country route used by Brigade 147 was extremely difficult for attached M48 tanks and other vehicles, most of which were lost trying to ford the Nhung River. The South Vietnamese and Americans thought that at least a reinforced North Vietnamese regiment held Highway 1 at Hai Lang and had engaged the fleeing South Vietnamese, halting all further movement to the south. The interdiction of the road by artillery and infantry weapons earned it the title "Highway of Horror" for the estimated 2,000 civilian and military dead left along one three-quarter mile stretch of road. One North Vietnamese soldier reported, "The people were moving on bicycles, motorbikes, and buses … No one was able to escape."

After long and heated discussion with his battalion commanders, Lieutenant-Colonel Nguyen Nang Bao established a tight perimeter for the night and planned to resume the march the next day. In the course of this, the brigade ascertained that all of its units were still organized and combat effective. But further to the south, Brigade 369 had been unsuccessful in keeping the road open between Quang Tri and Hue cities, although it had inflicted heavy losses on the communists and had not become pinned down in the effort. Brigade 369's goals were now directed at keeping the bridges across the O'Khe and My Chanh rivers open for withdrawing troops and civilians. Closely following Major Joy's radio traffic in order to effect a linkup during this mass exodus was Brigade 369's senior advisor, Major Robert Sheridan.

The last Fire Support base in Quang Tri Province, FSB Nancy, fell the next day, May 2. Lieutenant-General Le Nguyen Khang and the Marine Division headquarters were ordered by the Joint General Staff to assume command of all Marine units and to defend along the My Chanh River. Two Marine brigades, 147 and 369, were engaged with the enemy and the situation was confused as to who, and with what (if anything), was left to aid in the defense. Brigade 258 was still held in reserve, as Le Nguyen Khang, his staff, and advisors went into action defending Hue City.

Medical care in the field was available with basic first aid, while evacuation was required for more serious or complicated injuries. This depended on outside helicopter support, motor transport, or even river craft. (USMC)

In light of this crisis, the Vietnamese National Security Council met with President Nguyen Van Thieu and took drastic action to restore order.[12] Outside of Hue, military police units with highly visible sandbagged posts for firing squads alongside Highway 1 acted as a draconian reminder of duty for stragglers from Quang Tri City. The next day, Lieutenant-General Hoang Xuan Lam and his deputy were relieved, and on May 4, 1972 President Nguyen Van Thieu went to Hue to place Lieutenant-General Ngo Quang Truong in command of I Corps. Lieutenant-General Le Nguyen Khang was moved to the Joint General Staff as J-3 operations after turning down command of II Corps in MR 2. The Vietnamese Marine Division remained under his deputy, Colonel Bui The Lan, to hold the province, lost in part to American and Vietnamese interservice rivalry. For the first time since the invasion began, the Vietnamese Marine Division had its own area of operations. Even as they began digging in, the North Vietnamese continued building up their forces to attack toward Hue City. By May 6, 1972, the 3d Division could only account for 2,700 of its men and Brigadier-General Vu Van Giai was under arrest, to be later brought to trial, in part, for disobeying orders and abandoning a position in the face of the enemy. His defense was that with food, fuel, and ammunition gone he saw "no further reason why we should stay on in this ruined situation."

THE DEFENSE OF HUE CITY

South Vietnam reeled from the setbacks of the previous month. By May, the entire province of Quang Tri had fallen, and as a result the North Vietnamese would doggedly defend the Quang Tri Citadel for the next four and a half months. Elsewhere in MR 1, the NVA invaders threatened Hue City, occupying FSB Bastogne to the southwest, and the urban populace

12 Bong Song in MR 2 was captured by the NVA on May 3, 1972. The Paris Peace Talks were indefinitely suspended on May 4 by the American and South Vietnamese delegations.

was in a "near state of panic." In MR 3, just northwest of Saigon, NVA tanks rolled into An Loc and were held there by bitter fighting on the part of South Vietnamese forces. Both the United States and South Vietnam had to react to a crucial situation, and in less than a week the Americans responded with offshore forces and a build-up of air power in Vietnam. The US efforts included operations *Linebacker* bombing, *Freedom Train* naval gunfire, and *Pocket Money* mining of North Vietnam. These did not have an immediate effect on the communist offensive; the military tipping point for this effort came later. Equipment losses were staggering, but American tanks, howitzers, trucks, aircraft, and additional advisors soon arrived. In addition, personnel and equipment were provided from the USMC 1st ANGLICO, USMC 1st Radio Battalion, the USAF 20th Tactical Air Support Squadron, and the USA 14th Signal Company.[13]

HOLDING THE MY CHANH LINE

The abrupt changes in the MR 1 and FRAC structure were now in effect. Lieutenant-General Ngo Quang Truong moved his main command post to the Hue Citadel, reflecting the change in purpose and focus for operations. His first concerns were for the consolidation of the Hue City defenses, as well as reestablishing command and logistics structure. Ngo Quang Truong's available forces included the Marine and Airborne divisions responsible for

I Corps commander Lieutenant-General Ngo Quang Truong, ARVN, at his Hue City headquarters. (USMC)

the northern and northwestern areas of Thua Thien Province. The 1st Division was south and southwest of Hue City, and the 2d Division was in I Corp's southern provinces.

President Nguyen Van Thieu's orders were that the My Chanh Line would be held and there would be no further withdrawals. The Marine Division's battle line now extended from the Gulf of Tonkin, westward across Highway 1, and into the foothills. The division forward command post was moved from Hue City to the coastal village of Huong Dien. To support the division, elements of the Amphibious Support Battalion went from Saigon to the 1st Area Logistics Command at Hue. There Colonel Joshua Dorsey committed the entire staff of the advisory unit to provide critical combat operations, fire support coordination, and communications centers. The Marine battalion advisors were pulled back in favor of increased brigade advisory teams, and task organization provided battalion representation as needed, particularly for fire support.

The communist advance was halted at the My Chanh River, as everything to the north

13 On May 8, 1972, Haiphong and other North Vietnamese harbors were mined by the Seventh Fleet. At the same time, President Nixon offered to withdraw all US forces from Vietnam within four months of a formal ceasefire agreement.

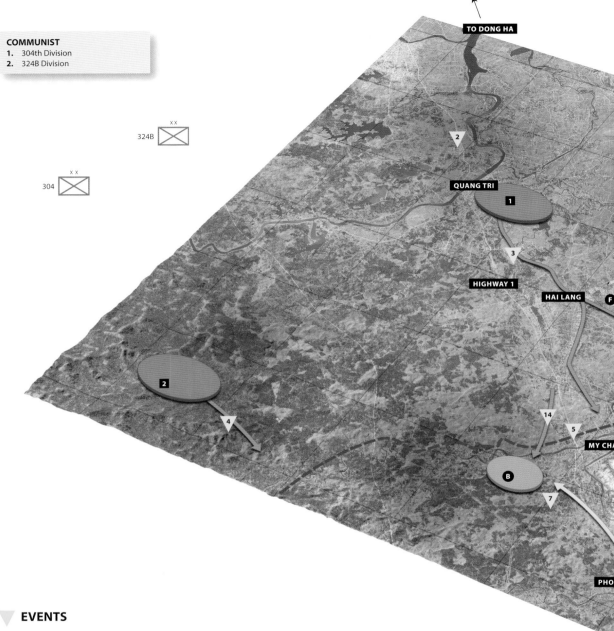

324B

304

TO DONG HA

QUANG TRI

HIGHWAY 1

HAI LANG

MY CHA

PHO

EVENTS

1. The VNMC Division's forward command post is moved from Hue City to the coastal village of Huong Dien.

2. The NVA holds Quang Tri Province with two divisions, freeing three divisions (304th, 308th, 324B) for further offensive operations against Hue City to the south.

3. The NVA 304th Division continues south along Highway 1.

4. Meanwhile, between May 2 and 25, the 324B Division strikes ARVN defenses in the west.

5. The communist advance is halted at the My Chanh River. Everything to the north is declared a free-fire zone.

6. May 5–25: The NVA probes the ARVN river-edge defenses, but the losses of the previous weeks do not permit any full-scale assaults. Artillery duels continue as the NVA efficiently uses its 130mm and 122mm guns, despite counter-fire from ARVN 175mm guns. NVA anti-aircraft artillery threat keeps Allied aircraft above 9,500ft.

7. Marine Brigade 258, under Lieutenant-Colonel Ngo Van Dinh, relieves Brigade 369 of responsibility for the western foothill approaches to the division.

8. 0930–1250hrs, May 13: Lieutenant-General Ngo Quang Truong launches the *Song Than* (*Tidal Wave*) operations. Helicopters from the US 9th Marine Amphibious

Brigade, Seventh Fleet, lift two battalions of Marine Brigade 369 into separate landings zones behind NVA lines.

9. The two Brigade 369 battalions attack to the south.

10. Meanwhile, a third Brigade 369 battalion crosses the My Chanh River heading north, catching the defending NVA regiment by surprise. Some 240 communists are killed, three tanks destroyed, and two artillery pieces put out of action.

11. May 21: The NVA responds with a full-scale tank–infantry attack, crossing the My Chanh River and heading straight into Brigade 369. As Regional Forces pull back, the Marines supported by ARVN armor and air strikes restore the line.

12. May 22: A further NVA tank–infantry attack follows on the brigade command post. Wire-guided missiles and LAW rockets destroy some NVA 10 tanks and armored vehicles. A Marine counter-attack restores the battle lines.

13. May 24: Brigade 147 lands by helicopter (two battalions) and amphibious tractors (one battalion) behind enemy lines.

14. May 25: The NVA responds with tank–infantry attacks on the My Chanh River Line, this time against Brigade 258. These continue the next day but are broken up by heavy artillery and air strikes.

Note gridlines are shown at intervals of 5km (3.1 miles)

THE DEFENSE OF HUE CITY, MAY 2–25, 1972

Hue City was a significant cultural and political center, and the loss of Quang Tri City proved a critical threat. As the focus to Military Region 1, it was defended at all costs. The efforts that followed ensured its protection, represented by its position as the forward I Corps headquarters.

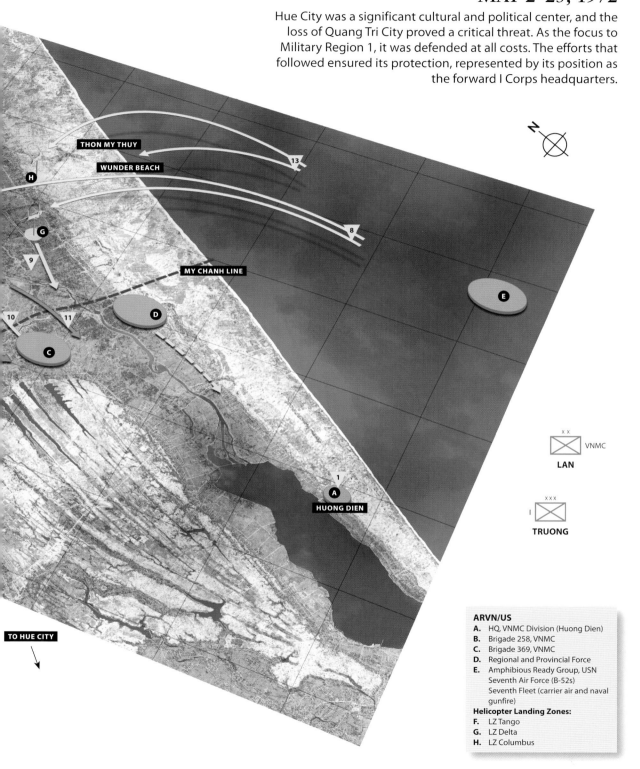

THON MY THUY

WUNDER BEACH

MY CHANH LINE

TO HUE CITY

HUONG DIEN

N

VNMC
LAN

I
TRUONG

ARVN/US
A. HQ, VNMC Division (Huong Dien)
B. Brigade 258, VNMC
C. Brigade 369, VNMC
D. Regional and Provincial Force
E. Amphibious Ready Group, USN
Seventh Air Force (B-52s)
Seventh Fleet (carrier air and naval gunfire)
Helicopter Landing Zones:
F. LZ Tango
G. LZ Delta
H. LZ Columbus

The Marine Division command post at Huong Dien, showing captured war materiel and some of the American (USA, USAF, USN, USMC) support personnel who provided communications, supporting-arms expertise, and equipment. (USMC)

VNMC Brigade 369 commander Lieutenant-Colonel Nguyen The Luong (right), standing next to Lieutenant-Colonel George E. Strickland (left). Another long-serving veteran, Luong was formerly the deputy chief of staff for operations and logistics. (Author's collection)

was declared a free-fire zone. The NVA would hold Quang Tri Province with two divisions, leaving three divisions (304th, 308th, 324B) for further offensive operations against Hue City to the south. From May 5 through 25, 1972, the NVA probed the ARVN river-edge defenses, but the losses of the previous weeks did not permit any full-scale assaults.[14] Artillery duels continued as the NVA efficiently used its 130mm and 122mm guns, despite counter-fire from ARVN 175mm guns. The NVA anti-aircraft artillery threat kept Allied aircraft to at least 9,500ft above ground level.

Marine Brigade 258, under Lieutenant-Colonel Ngo Van Dinh, relieved Brigade 369 of responsibility for the western foothill approaches to the division. Colonel Pham Van Chung's Brigade 369 could now concentrate on the eastern half of the division's area. In turn, Chung was promoted to division forward chief of staff as Lieutenant-Colonel Nguyen The Luong took over the brigade. With the defenses strengthened, a more active role was planned by I Corps.

14 The North Vietnamese launched major attacks on Kontum from May 14 to 25, 1972. At the international level, on May 19 Soviet and Chinese delegations traveled to Hanoi to discuss military support measures, while President Nixon went to Moscow on May 22.

THE MARINES ATTACK

Lieutenant-General Ngo Quang Truong used the Airborne and Marine divisions to conduct a series of limited raids and attacks using helicopter and amphibious assets near the coast. For the Marines this was with the *Song Than* (*Tidal Wave*) series of operations (*Song Than 5-72, 6-72, 8-72*) beginning on May 13, 1972 with a two-battalion raid supported by helicopters from the US 9th Marine Amphibious Brigade of the Seventh Fleet. The maximum lift capacity was used to bring Brigade 369 Marines into two separate landings zones behind enemy lines between 0930hrs and 1250hrs. The two battalions attacked to the south, while another battalion crossed the My Chanh River going north, catching the defending NVA regiment by surprise. Some 240 communists were killed, three tanks destroyed, and two artillery pieces put out of action.

The NVA responded thereafter with a full-scale tank-infantry attack on May 21, 1972, crossing the My Chanh River and heading straight into Brigade 369. As Regional Forces pulled back, the Marines supported by ARVN armor and air strikes restored the line. On May 22, 1972, a further NVA tank–infantry attack followed that closing on the brigade command post. Newly provided tube-launched, optically tracked, wire-guided (BGM-71 TOW) missile systems were used along with more ubiquitous LAW (M72 light anti-tank weapon) rockets to destroy some ten tanks and armored vehicles. The division G4 advisor, Major Robert D. Shoptaw, recalled advisors getting "a crash course on how to fire the LAW." A Marine counter-attack followed that restored the battle lines.

Brigade 147 followed next on May 24, 1972 with a helicopter and amphibious landing from Seventh Fleet's Amphibious Ready groups Bravo and Charlie, and the 9th Marine Amphibious Brigade. Fire support included B-52 Arc Light, artillery, and naval gunfire strikes. This time the landings were further behind enemy lines, a few miles southeast of Quang Tri City. Two battalions were lifted in by helicopter, while a third landed across the beach from amphibious tractors. Again, the NVA lost soldiers, supplies, and equipment, while 1,000 civilians were freed from communist control. For the second time in 11 days, the Marines were on the offensive.

The NVA again responded with tank–infantry attacks on the My Chanh River Line, this time against Brigade 258 on May 25, 1972. These continued the next

Troops move by UH-1E helicopters, providing mobility for otherwise foot-bound units. This was a force multiplier to allow the limited number of troops to serve at multiple locations. (USMC)

Helicopter support arriving from the 9th Marine Amphibious Brigade in 1972. Advisor Lieutenant-Colonel J.A. Poland guides a CH-46 in for a landing on a roadway landing zone at the counter-offensive's start. (USMC)

The 4th Marine Battalion helo-teams load USMC aircraft near Tan My. Previous training and experience led to smooth cooperation in air–ground operations. (*Marine Corps Gazette*)

day, but were broken up by heavy artillery and air strikes. The month of May had been a bad one for the communists, as they failed to capture Hue or dent the defense there. In the process, 2,960 soldiers were killed, 1,080 weapons were captured, and 64 armored vehicles destroyed or captured. During the same month, the Vietnamese Marines lost 209 killed and 637 wounded in action.

On May 28, 1972, President Nguyen Van Thieu promoted Lan to brigadier-general at the Imperial Palace in Hue. Command shifts continued, with Major-General Kroesen being replaced by Army Major-General Howard H. Cooksey at the FRAC and General Creighton Abrams being relieved by Army General Frederick C. Weyand as Commander, USMACV. By June, American military forces in South Vietnam reached a low of 49,000 personnel with the last combat units departing, although the US Marines had returned in some degree of strength with the shipboard 9th Marine Amphibious Brigade in the Gulf of Tonkin, Marine Aircraft Group 12 at Bien Hoa, and Marine Aircraft Group 15 at Da Nang, before moving to Nam Phong, Thailand.

IN THE BALANCE

Supporting armor, in the form of tanks and armored personnel carriers, came from the ARVN Armor Command. Marines ride here on an M41 tank near Bien Hoa. (USMC)

On June 8, 1972, Marines were sent north of the My Chanh under cover of B-52, tactical air, naval gunfire, and artillery strikes. Brigadier-General Bui The Lan's three Marine brigades crossed the My Chanh River in a major effort to shift the enemy from their defenses all along the line, while the NVA attempted to hold in depth along highways 1 and 555. American and South Vietnamese fire support played an important role to facilitate this and was much better integrated than in previous months. The NVA took a beating, as some 230 were killed, seven tanks destroyed, and weapons captured. According to the official history, "At the conclusion of the operation the Marines were north of the My Chanh River, once again in Quang Tri Province, and anxious to continue north."

South Vietnamese counter-offensives now began, as An Loc was relieved in MR 2 on June 18–19, 1972. Spoiling attacks in MR 1 continued into June, along with more aggressive planning by Lieutenant-General Ngo Quang Truong to

recapture Quang Tri at month's end. Limited NVA counter-attacks occurred but were far less coordinated or effective. The blood tax mounted to 4,475 NVA killed and 31 captured by Marines, who themselves suffered 1,480 casualties. According to G-3 advisor Lieutenant-Colonel Gerald Turley, "June ended with the Vietnamese Marine Corps at its peak combat strength. The infantry battalions were at their highest level ever. In addition, the VNMC recruit training center was operating at maximum capacity, and Marine recruiters had men waiting to enter the Corps." The division logistics posture was also excellent.

QUANG TRI CITY REDEEMED

With a firm hold on the southern portion of Quang Tri Province and daily attacking NVA supply lines, Lieutenant-General Ngo Quang Truong still had to defend Hue City against any further threats from the west while conducting offensive operations from positions along the My Chanh River to regain the Quang Tri City–Dong Ha area. According to generals Truong and Cooksey, a goal was the destruction of enemy forces and materiel that meant Quang Tri City could be at first bypassed. The Airborne and Marine divisions were to attack abreast, supported by surface and helicopter assaults to reach the Thach Han River. The Airborne Division was on the left flank with an area to include Highway 1 to the western foothills, with Quang Tri City in its zone of action. Its three brigades had previously been heavily engaged in MR 2 and were now assisted by US ANGLICO spot teams, along with their American army advisors. The Vietnamese Marine Division with three brigades was on the right flank with the task of destroying NVA units in order to assist in the recapture of Quang Tri City. The axis of advance would be along Route 555 taking in the area east to the coast. This effort

The 7th Marine Battalion on board Task Force 76 LCMs (landing craft mechanized) embarking for the landing across Wunder Beach in 1972. (*Marine Corps Gazette*)

The *Lam Son 72* counter-offensive, June 8–July 11, 1972

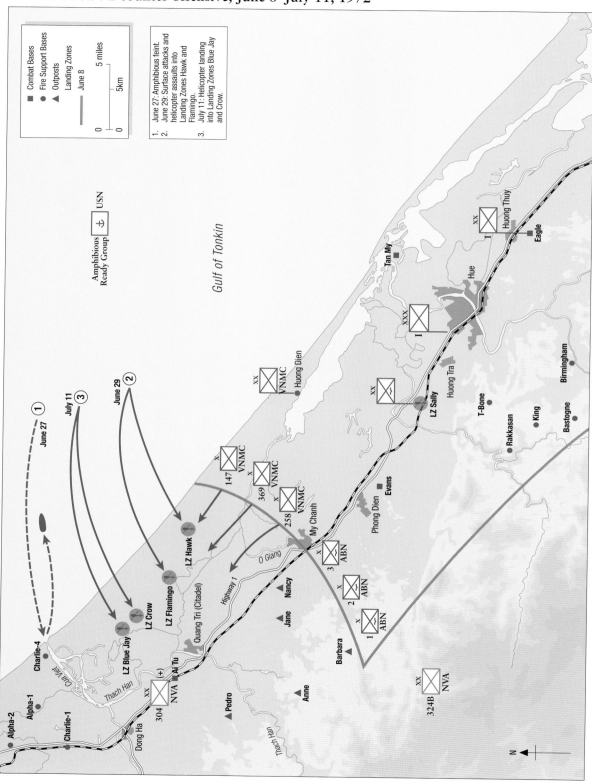

Legend:
- ■ Combat Bases
- ● Fire Support Bases
- ▲ Outposts
- ▲ Landing Zones
- June 8

Scale:
- 0 — 5 miles
- 0 — 5km

1. June 27: Amphibious feint.
2. June 29: Surface attacks and helicopter assaults into Landing Zones Hawk and Flamingo.
3. July 11: Helicopter landing into Landing Zones Blue Jay and Crow.

Amphibious Ready Group — USN

Gulf of Tonkin

June 27 ①
July 11 ③
June 29 ②

Charlie-4

Alpha-1
Alpha-2
Charlie-1

Dong Ha

304 XX
NVA
Ai Tu (+)

Thach Han
Cua Viet

LZ Blue Jay
LZ Crow
LZ Flamingo
Quang Tri (Citadel)
LZ Hawk

Pedro
Anne
Thach Han

Highway 1
O Giang

Jane
Nancy
Barbara

3 ABN x
2 ABN x
1 ABN x

324B XX
NVA

258 VNMC x
369 VNMC x
147 VNMC x
VNMC XX

My Chanh

Phong Dien
Evans

Huong Dien

LZ Sally
XX

XXX I

Hue
Huong Tra

Tan My

T-Bone
King
Rakkasan
Bastogne
Birmingham

1 XX
Huong Thuy
Eagle

N

US Army and Air Force advisors with the Airborne Division north of Camp Evans view the results of the American fire support. Despite this, the airborne was unable to advance, proof that light infantry needed more support. (Author's collection)

began with six days of combined supporting-arms fire and a naval feint at the mouth of the Cua Viet River by Seventh Fleet and its Amphibious Ready Groups using surface and heliborne forces. With this preparation, on June 28, 1972, I Corps launched the counter-offensive known as *Lam Son* (or *Total Victory*) 72.

The Marine Division's portion of the overall I Corps effort began on the same day, known to it as *Song Than 9-72*. Four battalions pushed north into heavy resistance. Brigadier-General Bui The Lan used a two-battalion helicopter assault on June 29, 1972 behind enemy lines in the vicinity of Wunder Beach to relieve pressure on the attacking units. For a third time, US Marine helicopters lifted the Vietnamese into enemy-held positions. Starting with shore, sea, and air attacks, including B-52 Arc Lights, the landings were conducted with precision against scattered resistance. As June ended, the NVA gave up more ground as it was pushed further north, leaving behind vehicles, dead, and prisoners. On June 30, President Nguyen Van Thieu went out to the USS *Blue Ridge* (LCC 19) to thank the American amphibious forces. Bui The Lan was also "appreciative of the superlative support provided the VNMC which enabled their offensive to be launched with such success."

The Airborne Division soon reached the Vinh Dinh River and the southern outskirts of Quang Tri City, despite resistance from well-entrenched communist units, and by July 4, 1972 was within 300 yards of the Citadel walls. This put the airborne units abreast of the Marines on July 7, but they were facing NVA forces determined to hold the city despite increasing artillery and air strikes. With the paratroopers mired in the city rubble, Bui The Lan was reluctant to expose an unprotected left flank by moving further north. By July 10, 1972, the five forward battalions of the Marine Division

OPPOSITE
With Hue City secured, the South Vietnamese launched their effort to return north. This involved surface and air movement to move forward against heavy opposition. Mobility provided by American forces allowed NVA flanks to be turned and the firepower to keep them isolated and pinned. The drive was led by the ARVN Airborne and Marine divisions. The Airborne had been weakened by previous heavy fighting and lacked the supporting structure of the Marines.

were on a line that ran from where Route 555 turned toward the city. Lan planned to maneuver two battalions from the west and east to hold the NVA in place, while a third battalion would helicopter in to block Route 560 from being used to resupply enemy forces in Quang Tri City.

VNMC Division supporting-arms schedule, July 11, 1972
Naval gunfire*

2400–0600hrs	2,400 rounds harassment and interdiction fires
0600–0800hrs	1,500 rounds preparation fires
0800–L-Hour	On-call direct-support fires
	(Two direct-support ships for VNMC Brigade 147 on D-1, three direct support ships as of 0800hrs D-Day)

Artillery

2400–0600hrs	Harassment and interdiction fires
0600–0800hrs	Preparation fires
0800–L-Hour	On-call direct-support fires

Tactical air

0800–1140hrs	Ten flights of tactical air
	(Six sorties of US aircraft with M84 bombs, two sorties of VNAF aircraft with CBU-55s—between third and fourth B-52 Arc Lights)
	One airborne US forward air controller (FAC) on station until 1900hrs**

On-call tactical air

1200–1230hrs	One sortie with bombs and napalm
1230–1300hrs	One sortie with bombs and napalm
1300–1900hrs	Two sorties per hour

Air Cavalry

	Command and control helicopter
	Two light observation helicopters
	Eight helicopter gunships
	Two search and rescue helicopters

Notes:

*	An alternate naval gunfire plan was developed for 0800–1140hrs should weather preclude the use of tactical air during this period.

**	A naval gunfire spotter was airborne with the FAC aircraft. The FAC was available to control air strikes if naval gunfire targets were not available; however, priority was given to naval gunfire missions in the objective area.

Vietnamese Marines aboard an ARVN M113 armored personnel carrier move north to recapture Quang Tri City. (USMC)

Artillery and air strikes on July 11, 1972 prepared the way for the air assault a mile and a quarter north of the city. This illustrates that Vietnamese efforts depended upon American fire support daily since March 1972. Between June and December 1972 alone, the Marine Division had used 3,992 American tactical air sorties and another 967 flown by the South Vietnamese. In addition, 525 B-52 strikes were flown in support to retake Quang Tri City. During this same period, 1,457,142 rounds of 105mm

Embarked on ship, the US Navy provides mess deck food that was a change from the usual diet encountered, in this case "a real stateside family style meal of pork cutlets and gravy, vegetables, and hot blue-berry pie" according to the original caption. (USMC)

shells were fired, along with 161,058 of 155mm or greater and 289,963 rounds of naval gunfire. This should be balanced against 2,971 enemy attacks by fire (artillery and mortars) expending an estimated 168,586 rounds of munitions.

American Marine helicopters lifted in 840 Vietnamese Marines into two landing zones and were immediately engaged by anti-aircraft artillery fire and SA-7 surface-to-air missiles, losing three aircraft in the process. Once on the ground, resistance was fierce with aircraft landing on a North Vietnamese tank and command post. Rapid support came from US Army AH-1 Cobra gunships and a counter-attack by the Marines that overran two trench lines to secure the landing zone from elements of the NVA 320B Division.

NAVY CROSS CITATION: LAWRENCE H. LIVINGSTON

Lawrence H. Livingston was recognized for actions as a captain on July 11, 1972. A native of Ohio, he was educated at Defiance College and Chapman College. Entering the USMC in 1960, he retired a major-general in 1997. During the attacks to regain Quang Tri City, the 1st Marine Battalion made a helicopter assault that required extraordinary effort to move forward under fire in the landing zone. Smith's repeated acts under direct fire were credited for this award. During the course of this he rescued a wounded ANGLICO naval gunfire spotter. His citation read:

For extraordinary heroism on 11 July 1972 while serving as Senior Advisory to the 1st VNMC Infantry Battalion during a heliborne assault into enemy-held territory northeast of Quang Tri City, Republic of Vietnam. When the battalion encountered unexpectedly heavy enemy fire while disembarking into the landing zone, and sustained numerous casualties, Captain Livingston moved throughout the hasty positions taken by the scattered and hesitant element and formed the Marines into an assault force. Despite the continuing heavy concentration of hostile fire, he began the assault on the initial objective—a tree line approximately 50 yards distant. Although blown from his feet by explosions and periodically delayed to reform and redirect his casualty-riddled force, he forged ahead, leading the Vietnamese Marines into the enemy-infested trench line, Captain Livingston shed his combat equipment, emerged from the trench line, and exposed himself to a hail of enemy fire to reach and carry his wounded naval gunfire spotter to a position of relative safety. Captain Livingston's repeated acts of heroism in the face of heavy fire reflected great credit upon him and the Marine Corps and were in keeping with the highest traditions of the United States Naval Service.

The Free World counter-offensive briefed by US Army and USMC staff, with Lieutenant-Colonel Gerald Turley at left, along with an air photo of the Quang Tri Citadel. The final objective was subject to debate, as it became a focus to be secured rather than an objective to be bypassed. (USMC)

During the next three days, with hand-to-hand fighting, the position was consolidated and the NVA fell back to the west toward Quang Tri City. Supporting Marine battalions overran an armored regiment's command post and numerous tracked vehicles and trucks were destroyed or captured. The G-3 advisor commented: "The execution was beautiful; lift off, staging, coordination, control, communications, prep fires—everything went on schedule," but at a cost and with courage.

To facilitate needed resupply, particularly of ammunition, Seventh Fleet provided a five-section floating causeway across Wunder Beach installed by US Navy "Seabees" and supervised by US Navy beachmaster and US Marine shore party personnel until the Vietnamese could assume control of the pier. Completed by July 13, 1972, it bypassed the battered Highway 1 line of communications.[15] By July 14, the Vietnamese Marines had cut the NVA's main supply line, Route 560, into Quang Tri City, which resulted for a time in diminished fighting. For the first time, US Army medical evacuation helicopters were able to clear the Marine casualties from the area, including Americans.

On July 17, 1972, the Marine Advisory Unit received needed replacements in Saigon from Fleet Marine Force Pacific. By July 20, the Marine Division

15 On July 13, 1972, the Paris Peace Talks resumed.

consolidated its hold on positions northeast of Quang Tri City as the Airborne Division continued efforts to retake the city. But little progress was made, with heavy fighting on both sides, despite the best NVA forces being "hashed up." For I Corps this became a problem, as now the city had become a major symbol, despite it not being a primary objective of the offensive. As a result of President Nguyen Van Thieu's concerns, Lieutenant-General Ngo Quang Truong had to plan and execute the capture of Quang Tri City and the Citadel. At the same time, Bui The Lan assigned Brigade 147 the task of moving north to drive the NVA across the Thach Han River or toward the Cua Viet River further north. On July 22, two battalions attacked north, supported by tanks and armored personnel carriers, while a third was landed by helicopters provided by the Americans. Despite entrenched resistance along Route 560, a linkup of these units was made by July 24, as some 133 communists were killed, five tanks or two armored vehicles captured, and a field hospital overrun.

By the end of the month, it was apparent to Ngo Quang Truong that the Airborne Division needed help, stalled 200 yards from the Citadel. During the night of July 27, 1972, Marine Brigade 258 relieved the ARVN paratroopers in place. The next four days witnessed heavy ground contact and artillery duels between the Marines and the North Vietnamese as Quang Tri City was defended by elements of the 308th, 312th, 320B, and 325th NVA divisions of the B5 Front. As the defense continued, these commands rotated units into the city, despite 1,880 casualties and the loss or destruction of 51 armored vehicles, seven anti-aircraft guns, four artillery pieces, 1,200 individual weapons, and 20 tons of munitions. The Brigade 258 advisor, Major Gordon W. Keiser, felt:

Brigade 369 advisors majors W.R. Hart and J.J. O'Brien consider their options in the ruins of Quang Tri City. (*Leatherneck* magazine)

Our chief advantage in supporting arms was air power, despite the high altitudes from which US aircraft were required to deliver ordnance as the war wound down. One day, another Marine advisor and I were directing air strikes on targets around the Quang Tri Citadel. Following several missions, the USAF forward air controller (airborne) [FAC (A)] told us he was going to try some "smart" ordnance, which was a brand-new concept at the time. After numerous drops, no bombs hit nearer than half a mile from its target. We asked the FAC (A) as to the cost of the many bombs expended … and advised him to go back to smart pilots and dumb bombs.

COMMUNIST
1. Elements of NVA 308th, 312th, 320B, and 325th divisions, B5 Front (total estimated strength of three regiments)
2. NVA artillery

320B

325 (+)

TO DONG HA

HIGHWAY 1

QUANG TRI AIRFIELD

8

2

AI TU COMBAT BASE

THACH HAN RI

QUANG

12

557

556

▼ EVENTS

1. By July 4, the Airborne Division has reached the southern outskirts of Quang Tri City and is within 300 yards of the Citadel walls, but facing determined NVA defenders.

2. By July 10, the five forward battalions of the VN Marine Division are on a line running from where Route 555 (nicknamed "Triple Nickel") turns toward the city.

3. July 11: 840 Vietnamese Marines are helicoptered in to block Route 560 from being used to resupply enemy forces in Quang Tri City, landing at zones Lima and Victor. The LZs are secured from elements of the NVA 320B Division, which fall back to the west toward Quang Tri City.

4. By July 14, the Vietnamese Marines have cut the NVA's main supply line, Route 560, into Quang Tri City.

5. The Airborne Division continues efforts to retake the city, but despite heavy fighting, little progress is made, stalling 200 yards from the Citadel.

6. July 22: Brigade 147 attacks north to drive the NVA across the Thach Han River and along Route 560.

7. July 27, night: VNMC Brigade 258 relieves the ARVN paratroopers in place. In August, it moves slowly forward, fighting house to house in the Citadel.

8. NVA artillery continues to target South Vietnamese forces from north and west of the Thach Han River, particularly around the Ai Tu Combat Base.

9. August 22: a sizable enemy force attempts to break out from the Citadel; the surprised 8th Marine Battalion manages to drive the attack back. With river crossings held on both Highway 1 and Route 560, all NVA supply and infiltration routes are effectively blocked.

10. September 8: 1st Ranger Group relieves Brigade 147 from its blocking positions north of the city. Brigadier-General Bui The Lan begins an all-out assault on Quang Tri City, with Brigade 258 attacking in the south and Brigade 147 from the northeast, supported by intensive artillery and air strikes.

11. September 10, night: Lieutenant-Colonel Do Huu Tung's 6th Marine Battalion secures the southeast wall and by the next morning has a company inside the Citadel. Meanwhile, the 3d and 7th Marine battalions fight their way through the northern part of the city and reach the north wall.

12. September 11–15: other VNMC battalions cross the Thach Han River, despite NVA counter-attacks.

13. By 1700hrs, September 15, the Marines are in complete control of the Citadel, ending the 138-day communist occupation.

THE QUANG TRI CITY BATTLES, JULY 22–SEPTEMBER 16, 1972

The continued advantage of American fire and maneuver support allowed the ARVN assault on Quang Tri City. Both Airborne and Marine divisions closed on the walls of the Quang Tri Citadel in early July, but a final victory against the NVA would not follow until mid-September 1972.

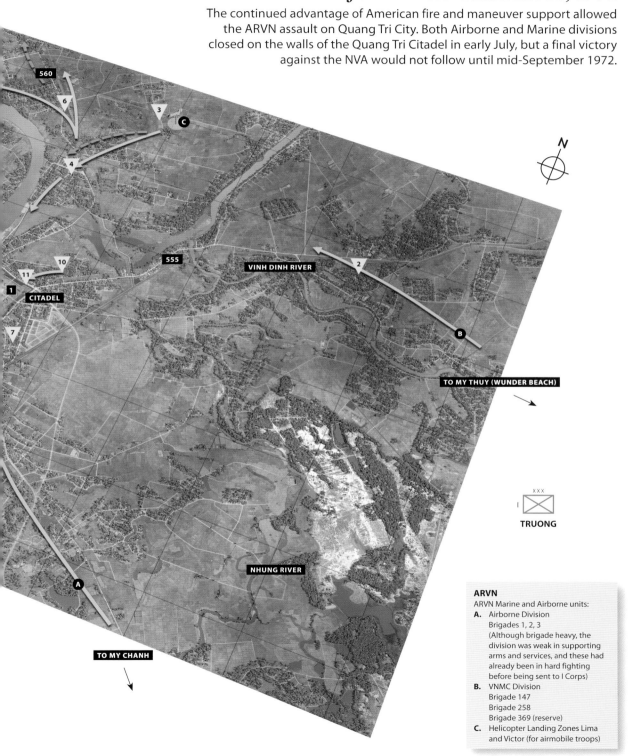

560

6

3

C

4

10

555

11

1

CITADEL

7

VINH DINH RIVER

2

B

TO MY THUY (WUNDER BEACH)

N

TRUONG

xxx

A

NHUNG RIVER

TO MY CHANH

ARVN
ARVN Marine and Airborne units:
A. Airborne Division
Brigades 1, 2, 3
(Although brigade heavy, the division was weak in supporting arms and services, and these had already been in hard fighting before being sent to I Corps)
B. VNMC Division
Brigade 147
Brigade 258
Brigade 369 (reserve)
C. Helicopter Landing Zones Lima and Victor (for airmobile troops)

A Vietnamese Marine and his advisor, Captain A.J. Livingston, admire their efforts in field cooking. A more common eating experience, at times this produced good results relying on rice and nuoc mam sauce. (USMC)

As August began, most of Quang Tri City remained in communist hands. The territory north and west of the Thach Han River, particularly around the Ai Tu Combat Base, was dotted with NVA artillery positions. The enemy continued a seemingly endless barrage of artillery and mortar fire on the South Vietnamese. This required ground units digging in "like gophers" and counter-battery efforts by artillery, naval gunfire, and Allied aircraft. Keiser recalled, "NVA artillery, especially the 130mm and 122mm guns, was quite effective. It was rapid; it was accurate; it was terrifying." To take pressure off the city, in MR 1 on August 18–19, 1972 the NVA 711th Division attacked Que Son and captured FSB Ross from the South Vietnamese, while continuing to threaten Da Nang into the next month.

The Marine Division headquarters, located close to the action, allowed brigade commanders to direct tactical actions within their area of operations, while providing responsive command and control of all supporting arms. The brigades of the division were well placed to deny the NVA resupply and to make a final lunge into the heart of Quang Tri City—the Citadel—but were held up by the concealed defenders. Enemy fire and the congestion of friendly units in the area severely hampered maneuver by the Marines. The continued slow progress saw Brigadier-General Bui The Lan looking for ways to reinforce the maneuver units to overpower the estimated three regiments of NVA defenders. Brigade 147, operating northeast of the city, began receiving heavy pressure from the enemy, but had prevented any efforts to reopen Route 560. The blockade of supplies began to take its toll on the NVA's ammunition stockpiles. All enemy resupply made its way into the city ferried across the Thach Han River. To the south, Brigade 258 with four battalions was house-to-house fighting within Quang Tri City. Each day the brigade moved slowly forward and tightened its grasp on the communist forces still in the Citadel. Brigade 369 was the division reserve.

On August 22, 1972, a sizable enemy force attempted a breakout from the Citadel. Before the attack, a curtain of artillery fire hit the 8th Marine Battalion and the NVA infantry advanced behind the cover of tanks. The surprised Marines rallied and drove the attack back. For the remainder of the month, a continued series of increasingly desperate night attacks were made to rupture the tight circle the Marines had drawn. By this time in the invasion and counter-offensive, the Vietnamese Marines had suffered 1,670 men killed and 4,914 wounded. The American Marine advisors would suffer 14 casualties in the end. During the same five-month period, the Marines estimated they had killed 10,279 communists.

As September began, the Marine Division had been in constant street fighting inside the city for 35 days under some of the heaviest shelling since the invasion began (more than 50,000 rounds of artillery and mortar fire). Located inside the city were the 1st, 3d, 5th, 6th, and 8th Marine battalions dealing with local counter-attacks. River crossings were held on both Highway 1 and Route 560 as all enemy supply and infiltration routes were effectively blocked and the communists felt the bite of food supply and ammunition shortages. On September 8, 1972, the 1st Ranger Group relieved Brigade 147 from its blocking positions north of the city. This gave Brigadier-General Bui The Lan two brigades to begin an all-out assault on the city, with Brigade 258 attacking in the south and Brigade 147 from the northeast. Generals Truong and Lan also asked for a Seventh Fleet diversion from the sea in support of this.

THE FINAL ASSAULT ON QUANG TRI CITADEL

On September 9, 1972, intensive artillery and air strikes began on the Citadel. Along with this was the feint north of the Cua Viet River by Task Force 76 and the 9th Marine Amphibious Brigade. Heavy naval gunfire and air strikes prepared the beach area that was approached by landing craft and helicopters, which then turned away at the last minute. During this the Marine Division advanced rapidly, taking advantage of the NVA's distraction. The boundary for brigades 258 and 147 divided the Citadel in half, with one brigade advancing from the north and the other from the south. The walls of the antiquated brick fortification were 15ft thick and 15ft high; although portions were reduced to rubble, other areas were tunneled and formed an intricate system of interlocking defensive positions. The evening of September 9 saw the 3d and 7th Marine battalions held short of the northern wall, while the 6th Battalion reached the southeast bastion. That night, Lieutenant-Colonel Do Huu Tung was able to get a squad inside and back out of the Citadel.

During the night of September 10, 1972, Lieutenant-Colonel Tung's 6th Marine Battalion launched an assault on the southeast wall and secured the top, and by the next morning had a platoon, then later a company, inside the Citadel. The 1st and 2d Marine battalions moved to support the 6th Battalion while the 3d and 7th Marine battalions fought their way through the northern part of the city and reached the north wall. While these actions occurred, other VNMC battalions crossed the Thach Han River, despite NVA

The fight continues at the walls of the Quang Tri Citadel. This became the focus of the counter-offensive and the critical goal for the Marines. (VNMC)

counter-attacks from September 11 to 15. On September 15, at 1015hrs, the 3d Marine Battalion also forced an entry into the Citadel as massive and desperate NVA artillery barrages were called in on the position. The NVA considered this a "meat grinder" and a "land of death," with no place for their revolutionary forces. By 1700hrs, the Marines were in complete control of the Citadel. After being occupied by the communists for 138 days, at 1245hrs, on September 16, 1972, the 6th Battalion raised the South Vietnamese striped red and yellow flag over the fort's west gate. This was a defining victory for the Vietnamese Marine Corps and American advisors. The official US Marine Corps history of the period recorded: "The Vietnamese Marine Division, with its victory at Quang Tri City, had come of age as a fighting unit."

For its actions through September 19, 1972, the Chief of the Joint General Staff of the RVNAF General Cao Van Vien issued an official order recognizing the Vietnamese Division for its efforts to recapture Quang Tri City with the Unit Citation Fourragère and Badge in the color of the Cross of Gallantry with Palm. The unit award included supporting Allied forces, as it appeared that victory had been recovered from defeat.[16] The senior American advisor in I Corps felt that "the tactical results of the fight to take Quang Tri City and the ancient Citadel are impressive and have created a great psychological and moral victory over the invaders."

On September 20, 1972, President Nguyen Van Thieu arrived at the Vietnamese Division to congratulate Brigadier-General Bui The Lan and

16 On April 14 and May 7, 1973, awards were made to Amphibious Force, US Seventh Fleet and the 9th Marine Amphibious Brigade for their active part in the campaign.

the Marines for their effort. He then made his way to Brigade 147 and 6th Marine Battalion. During the seven-week battle to recapture Quang Tri City, the Vietnamese Marines suffered 3,658 casualties of those sustained since June, a quarter of the entire corps.

Up and over by the 6th Marine Battalion, and the 3d, as they push the NVA out of positions in the Citadel. Despite resistance, the Marines were able to secure their assigned military and political objective. (VNMC)

RETURNING NORTH

On September 25, the South Vietnamese positions were consolidated as Brigade 369 assumed operational control of Quang Tri City from Hai Lang. Brigade 147 assumed control of the positions along the coast on the division's right flank, while Brigade 258 reverted to division reserve. The ARVN Airborne Division continued to operate further west along the Marines' flank. For the South Vietnamese, the battle was far from over for the remainder of the province. Assistance and security had to be provided to the civilians in reoccupied areas using the territorial Regional and Popular forces, allowing the return of a major portion of the province population to the Republic of Vietnam.

Communist artillery fire from the northwest continued to strike Marine positions daily, sometimes followed by nighttime probing attacks. Enemy activity dropped sharply after the taking of Quang Tri City, but it was evident the NVA was still present in strength just outside the city. Identification of units from the NVA 312th Division raised the total to six divisions in Quang Tri Province as reported by FRAC. Heavy monsoon rains began to

STORMING THE QUANG TRI CITADEL, SEPTEMBER 15, 1972 (PP. 78–79)

The storming of the Quang Tri Citadel, which began on September 9, 1972, was hard fought by infantry on both sides, and had symbolic as well as military value. Taking place within the tactical zones of 147 and 258 VNMC brigades on September 15, 1972, the VNMC 6th Marine Battalion was recognized for the achievement. Bragging rights were disputed between elements of the 3d Marine Battalion as to who entered the Citadel first.

The Citadel was divided as an objective, with VNMC Brigade 147 on the left (or north) and Brigade 258 on the right (or south). This was perhaps intended to give either unit the chance of success in taking the Citadel, or to create competition instead of cooperation. Entry was gained at two points by night infiltration and attacks, one of which is shown here on September 15. This still allowed remaining NVA troops to pull out before the final capture of the Citadel the following day.

Shown here are soldiers from the Vietnamese Marines in their "tiger stripe" camouflage uniforms (**1**). They are armed with M16 rifles (**2**); to the right, a machine gunner provides covering fire with an M60 (**3**). The Marine to the left has an M18 Colored Smoke Grenade attached to his right chest, and on his right shoulder can be seen the VNMC sleeve insignia (**4**). The darkness is illuminated by flares (**5**) and tracer fire. The heavily destroyed state of the 19th-century Citadel is clear (**6**), the result of earlier fighting for the city; the rubble provided strong defensive positions for the communist troops from which they could hold off the attacking Marines.

fall in October 1972. Torrential downpours made passage impossible in the low-lying coastal marshlands, particularly for artillery and armor. With the declining weather, the enemy proximity, continued American support, and the possibility of a ceasefire halt, Brigadier-General Bui The Lan sought to improve his position on the ground with a limited offensive.

Colonel Nguyen Nang Bao's VNMC Brigade 147 on the division eastern flank was ordered to attack up Route 560 between the Thach Han and Vinh Dinh rivers to push the NVA back beyond mortar range and to recapture the Trien Phong District headquarters. Artillery, naval gunfire, and tactical air support for the 8th Marine Battalion began on October 7, 1972 prior to H-Hour. Poor weather and enemy resistance delayed the attack until October 10, 1972, at which point Lieutenant-Colonel Nguyen Nang Bao had his battalions on-line and succeeded in cutting the NVA supply route. The result was 111 enemy killed and 55 weapons captured. On October 20, 1972, Nguyen Nang Bao was to conduct an infantry and armor attack with the 9th Marine Battalion to reach the Cua Viet River. Again, this took place against determined resistance, including the use of 122mm rockets. Meanwhile, Lieutenant-Colonel Nguyen The Luong and VNMC Brigade 369 held the western portion of the division front through the first part of the month, experiencing daily artillery fire. Ground movement was limited to patrolling and defensive works. Colonel Ngo Van Dinh's Brigade 258 remained the division's reserve. By month's end, the front stabilized to the point that control of the mouth of the Cua Viet River was in their hands.

Advisor Captain H.L. Reed and Vietnamese Marines deployed in the field on operations near Nam Can. A map and compass is needed for land navigation, one of the chores that indicated an advisor's tactical competency. (*Marine Corps Gazette*)

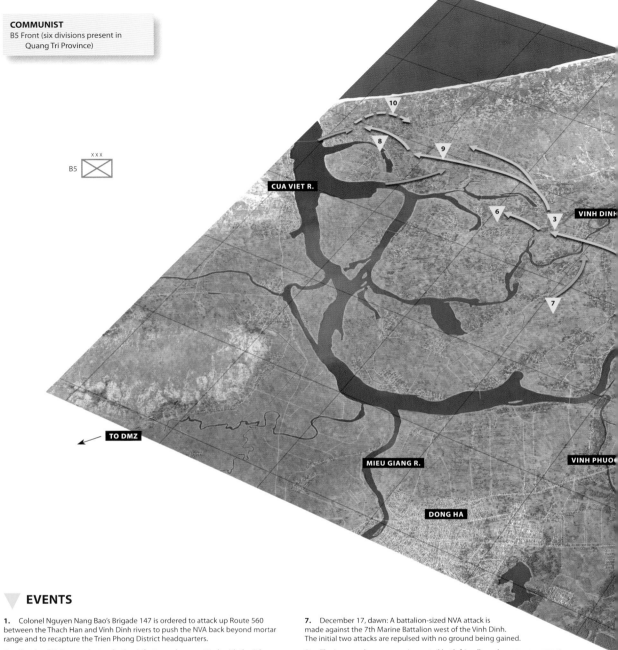

B5

CUA VIET R.

VINH DINH

TO DMZ

MIEU GIANG R.

VINH PHUOC

DONG HA

EVENTS

1. Colonel Nguyen Nang Bao's Brigade 147 is ordered to attack up Route 560 between the Thach Han and Vinh Dinh rivers to push the NVA back beyond mortar range and to recapture the Trien Phong District headquarters.

2. October 20: Bao conducts a further infantry and armor attack with the 9th Marine Battalion to reach the crucial artery of the Cua Viet River. It faces determined communist resistance.

3. By month's end the front has stabilized, and South Vietnamese forces are nearing the mouth of the Cua Viet River.

4. November 1: Some 600 men of the 6th Marine Battalion, Brigade 369 cross the Thach Han River opposite the Quang Tri Citadel. The next day the Marine advance has become bogged down by NVA resistance some 550 yards beyond the riverbank.

5. During the hours of darkness on November 2–3, the 6th Marine Battalion breaks contact and withdraws to the east, leaving a reconnaissance team on the west bank.

6. November 11: The 4th Marine Battalion moves to the northwest, but NVA mortar and artillery fire, along with local counterattacks, prevent them from reaching the Cua Viet River. The front lines generally remain static until mid-December, with only company-sized NVA attacks.

7. December 17, dawn: A battalion-sized NVA attack is made against the 7th Marine Battalion west of the Vinh Dinh. The initial two attacks are repulsed with no ground being gained.

8. The increased monsoon rains curtail both friendly and enemy movement. A B-52 strike in support of the 4th Marine Battalion south of the Cua Viet River on the coast takes out six significant hill-masses.

9. Brigadier-General Bui The Lan plans a final effort prior to a certain ceasefire, to be launched January 26, 1973. The objective is the mouth of the Cua Viet River, where a previous RVN naval base and C4 combat outpost dominates the river mouth. The assigned Task Force Tango is led by Colonel Nguyen Than Tri, the deputy commandant of the VNMC. The route of advance is along the beach in two parallel columns. The NVA offers a strong frontal defense, and its counter-attacks aim at cutting off the VNMC lines of advance and retreat.

10. The final assault is made on January 28 by a mixed force from the 3d, 4th, and 5th Marine battalions. At 0745hrs this same day, USS *Turner Joy* (DD 951) fires the last naval gunfire mission of the war. The ceasefire goes into effect at 0800hrs. The fighting continues at the mouth of the Cua Viet River as the NVA counter-attack. By January 30, the Marines are encircled, and a post-ceasefire breakout takes place on January 31.

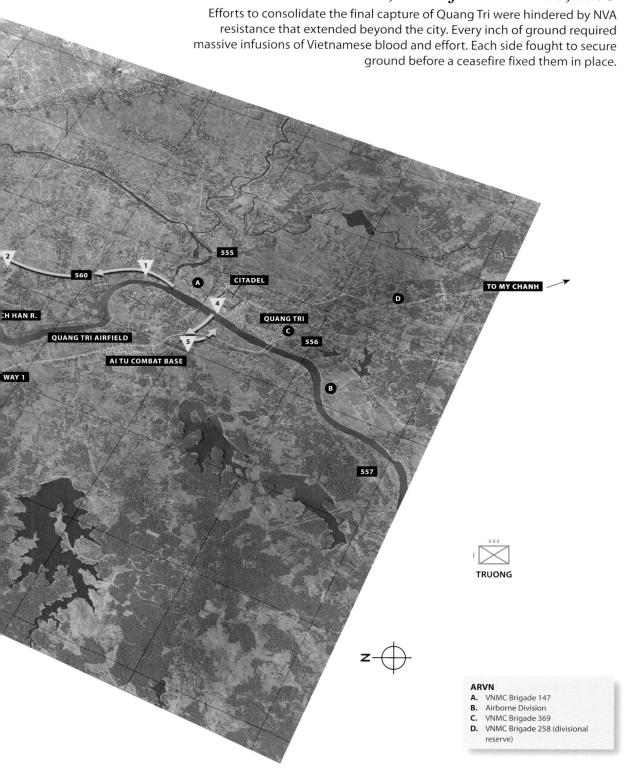

Note gridlines are shown at intervals of 2.5km (1.55 miles)

FINAL DEPLOYMENT OF FORCES, SEPTEMBER 17, 1972–JANUARY 30, 1973

Efforts to consolidate the final capture of Quang Tri were hindered by NVA resistance that extended beyond the city. Every inch of ground required massive infusions of Vietnamese blood and effort. Each side fought to secure ground before a ceasefire fixed them in place.

2

560

1

555

A

CITADEL

D

TO MY CHANH

CH HAN R.

4

QUANG TRI

QUANG TRI AIRFIELD

C

5

556

AI TU COMBAT BASE

WAY 1

B

557

TRUONG

Z

ARVN
A. VNMC Brigade 147
B. Airborne Division
C. VNMC Brigade 369
D. VNMC Brigade 258 (divisional reserve)

THE ELEVENTH HOUR

As replacements filled the depleted division ranks, commensurate with operations, the battalions were rotated out of the line in order to conduct training and inspections near Wunder Beach. Basic skills and knowledge were demonstrated in an area only 4 miles from the fighting. This included control of tactical air and naval gunfire by US Marines of Sub Unit One, 1st ANGLICO.

On November 1, 1972, Brigade 369 was ordered to move the division area of control in the west. Some 600 men of the 6th Marine Battalion crossed the Thach Han River across from the Quang Tri Citadel. The improvised crossing in flooded conditions was difficult as guide ropes broke and sampans overturned. By the next day, up to 400 Marines advanced only to become bogged down by NVA resistance some 550 yards beyond the riverbank. Efforts to move north along Highway 1 were stopped by an NVA regiment supported by mortars and artillery. With all company commanders killed and some 40 Marines missing, during the hours of darkness on November 2–3 the battalion broke contact and withdrew to the east, leaving a reconnaissance team on the west bank. The 4th Marine Battalion moved to the northwest on November 11, 1972 (the day after the US Marine Corps' 197th birthday). Again, mortar and artillery fire, along with local counter-attacks, kept them from reaching the Cua Viet River.

The front lines generally remained static, with the VNMC no closer than 3½ miles from the Cua Viet River. During the first part of December 1972, the NVA initiated nothing larger than company-sized attacks. Then, on December 17, a battalion-sized attack was made against the 7th Marine Battalion west of the Vinh Dinh Canal. The initial two attacks were repulsed with 37 killed, and another 132 communist casualties on the next day, with no ground being gained. The increased monsoon rains now curtailed both friendly and enemy movement. Transporting supplies was difficult for both sides, and fire missions were less likely as targets were located in the shared miserable conditions. An exception was a B-52 strike in support of the 4th Marine Battalion south of the Cua Viet River on the coast. The bomb load took out six significant hill masses instead of the three targeted. Those NVA who survived the attack moved back into their battered positions afterward. December 1972 was characterized by the ever-present possibility that the continued negotiations between American National Security Advisor Henry Kissinger and North Vietnam's representative Le Duc Tho would result in a ceasefire accord and that a truce agreement would go into effect. As 1973 began, both sides below the DMZ made probes and counter-probes.

By January 14, 1973, battalions of brigades 147 and 258 experienced heavy contact all

Vietnamese Marines conduct basic combat skills training, seen with this battalion mortar squad. Sure that the war was not finished, they prepared for further combat. This was a distinctive focus for the Marines. (*Leatherneck* magazine)

along the front, as steps were taken to withdraw remaining US military personnel from MR 1. On January 15, Brigadier-General Bui The Lan was ordered to make another effort to cross the mouth of the Cua Viet River prior to a certain ceasefire. A measure of its importance is indicated by the fact that the assigned Task Force Tango was led by Colonel Nguyen Than Tri, the deputy commandant of the VNMC. On January 26, 1973, a ground attack was launched with two mechanized columns and the fire of all available supporting arms. Despite determined NVA resistance, initial objectives were seized on the line of advance along the coast and a route 1½ miles inland. The final assault was made on January 28, 1973 by a mixed force from the 3d, 4th, and 5th Marine battalions, but the enemy disabled some 25 or so M48

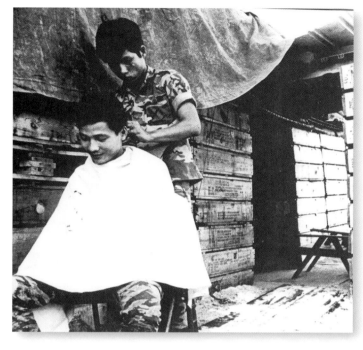

Vietnamese Marines regrouped during the fall of 1972 and recovered from the previous months of combat. Laundry and haircuts made the top of the list of required actions. Little did they know that more combat would follow quicker than expected. (*Leatherneck* magazine)

tanks and M113 armored personnel carriers with ATGMs, and air support was kept at a distance by SA-7 surface-to-air missiles. At 0745hrs, that day, the USS *Turner Joy* (DD 951) fired the last naval gunfire mission of the war, and the Americans withdrew all further support as the ceasefire went into effect at 0800hrs. Without direct American support, the Marines stalled in the face of heavy resistance, and for Task Force Tango the fighting continued at the mouth of the Cua Viet as the NVA counter-attacked. By January 30, 1973, the Marines were encircled and unable to secure their final objective or obtain resupply. Some 40 casualties and 20 armored vehicles were lost by the 4th Marine Battalion in the post-ceasefire breakout on January 31.

The front line remained at the Thach Han River, leaving parts of Quang Tri Province under communist occupation with the ceasefire and American withdrawal. With the need to move further north, these efforts failed. A communist flag flies on the northern bank, with nationalist flags in the foreground. (VNMC)

AFTERMATH

The victory at Quang Tri City celebrated by the Marines and Republic of Vietnam with displays of captured equipment and other trophies. For the Vietnamese and American Marine advisors this was a material reminder of their success. Once more, the Marines had defeated the communists on the battlefield. (Author's collection)

THE FINAL ACT

Along with these tactical events, outside strategic policies and factors were in play. President Nixon had used diplomatic and military pressure to bring about the settlement of the war as the South Vietnamese fought to regain lost territory and the aerial bombing and mining of North Vietnam took effect. From September 26–27, 1972, private talks continued in Paris between Henry Kissinger and Le Duc Tho. By October 8, 1972, Kissinger announced a "breakthrough" in the peace talks. By October 11, 1972, the combined efforts had closed the ports through which North Vietnam obtained 85 percent of its foreign trade, with imports cut from over 250,000 tons a month to almost zero. By then, US authorities believed the communist politburo wanted to reach an agreement. On October 19–20, 1972, Kissinger presented the "breakthrough" agreement to South Vietnamese President Nguyen Van Thieu during discussions in Saigon. As a peace gesture by the Americans, on October 23, 1972, US Armed Forces stopped air and naval gunfire bombardment north of the 20th Parallel. Elections held in the United States witnessed Richard M. Nixon's defeat of George S. McGovern on November 7, 1972. During the same month, US Army direct participation in the Vietnam War ended as the remaining American bases were turned over to the South Vietnamese.

Despite apparent agreement, the peace talks stalled as private talks continued in November and December 1972, among false starts and recriminations by both parties and their allies. President Nixon warned that bombing would resume if an agreement did not result. He subsequently authorized Operation *Linebacker II* on December 18, 1972 when the North Vietnamese failed to act in good faith on previous ceasefire proposals, opening the way for the Christmas bombing of Hanoi and the virtual destruction

Communist-controlled areas of South Vietnam, 1973

Communist-controlled areas

0   50 miles
0   50km

N

Demilitarized Zone (DMZ)

Tchepone

Dong Ha
Quang Tri
Hue

Da Nang
Hoi An

South China Sea

LAOS

I CORPS

THAILAND

Chavane

Chu Lai
Quang Ngai

Attacu

Dak To
Kontum

Siem Pang
Pleiku

Qui Nhon

Mekong River

CAMBODIA

II CORPS

Tuy Hoa

Tonle
Sap

Kratie

Nha Trang

Loc Ninh
Da Lat

Phum Krek
An Loc

Phnom Penh

Tay Ninh
III CORPS

Svay
Rieng

Bien Hoa
Saigon

Phan Tiet

Tan Chau

Cao Lanh
My Tho
Vung Tao

Rach Gia
Can Tho

IV CORPS

Gulf of Thailand

South China Sea

Quan Long
(Ca Mau)

PREVIOUS PAGE
In the end, the North Vietnamese communists held portions of South Vietnam despite efforts to force them out. International recognition did nothing to prevent this. As such, the war continued against these incursions. The situation was set for the final South Vietnamese defeat in 1975.

of critical targets in the north. The intensity of operations was unmatched by any of the previous eight years of strikes against North Vietnam and *Linebacker II*'s blows brought the communists back to the negotiating table. This produced results by the New Year.

The Agreement on Ending the War and Restoring Peace in Vietnam met both American and North Vietnamese demands that had evolved during the course of the conflict. It was a unilateral accord that called for the cessation of all military operations in Vietnam to go into effect at 2400hrs GMT, January 27, 1973. Military operations in Vietnam ceased on January 28, but continued in Laos until February 21, 1973 and Cambodia until August 15, 1973. All forces would remain in place, with disengagement supervised by a Two-Party Joint Military Commission, and only the replacement of existing equipment and supplies. Within 60 days, all Americans would withdraw, all prisoners of war would be returned, and all US mines would be cleared from North Vietnam waterways. It did not consider the ongoing relations between the Republic of Vietnam and the Provisional Revolutionary Government of the communists in South Vietnam. The Ceasefire Campaign was over.

For the Vietnamese of both sides, the struggle continued, fought hard from the morning of the ceasefire and for a month or two thereafter. The communists throughout South Vietnam raised the starred blue and red flags of the National Liberation Front. In a land-grab effort just prior to the ceasefire, expecting the government forces to be hampered by the terms and timing of the agreement, these communist attacks continued through to the end. The South Vietnamese countered with military attacks during and after the ceasefire, which were successful in defending the territory they already held. While the major American equipment and resupply ended with the ceasefire, NVA infiltration continued. This included numbers of armored vehicles and artillery moved into base areas in South Vietnam. Although

Allied senior leadership in Saigon: (from left to right, front to rear) American President Richard M. Nixon and Vietnamese President Nguyen Van Thieu; American advisor Henry Kissinger, Vietnamese Vice President Nguyen Cao Ky, and American Ambassador Ellsworth Bunker. (US Army)

the ARVN and NVA had equal numbers of vehicles inside the south, the North Vietnamese had twice as many trained crews. Similar build-ups were witnessed in artillery and anti-aircraft weapons that countered South Vietnamese air superiority.

VICTORY FROM DEFEAT, 1972

Both the ARVN and the USMACV claimed that the VNMC played a major part in the battlefield defeat that resulted in the loss of Quang Tri City and Province. This was based on two observations: (1) Vietnamese Marines paid more attention to their service leaders than their tactical commanders, and (2) the demands from the Vietnamese Marine leaders and their American Marine advisors to fight for the first time as a division command.

The actions and motivation of the Vietnamese Marines were subjected to various interpretations: 3d Division senior advisor Colonel Donald Metcalf stated the VNMC lost Quang Tri City; FRAC's Major-General Kroesen implied it; and USMACV's General Abrams' ire was directed against both the VNMC and ARVN armored units—at least until he departed Vietnam in June 1972, which coincided with the beginning of the successful counter-offensive to regain both the province and city by the VNMC and ARVN Airborne divisions supported by American air and naval forces.

As early as 1974, Australian Army Brigadier Francis P. Serong repeated claims of VNMC misconduct, similar to those made by ARVN and US Army personnel. US Army General William C. Westmoreland even commented on this in his memoirs in 1976. One of the Marine advisors' most vocal

After the 1972 conflict, Vietnamese military historians meet with US Marine Corps Director of History and Museum Colonel (Ret.) John W. Ripley at the Washington Navy Yard in the process of exchanging records and recovering remains. Like the author, some of the Vietnamese were veterans of the 1972 fighting. (Author's collection)

defenders, Lieutenant-Colonel Gerald Turley, created additional debate in a 1985 book that continued to fuel the unsubstantiated charges of Vietnamese Marine misbehavior more than a decade after the debacle.

In an interesting final note, Major-General Kroesen felt the North Vietnamese's inability to pursue and destroy routed South Vietnamese forces was evidence that, if defended, Quang Tri City would not have fallen. The communists did not have the resources or organization to do what the ARVN forces had done to themselves with American counsel. Claims arose that Marine Brigade 147's withdrawal on May 1, 1972 caused the collapse of Quang Tri City, even though the unit was the last to leave and stayed long enough for the division commander and his army advisors to escape. The brigade actually maintained itself as an effective force by saving lives and equipment, the same logic presented by Brigadier-General Vu Van Giai at his court martial. Real questions should have been directed at the performance of ARVN units, particularly the 2d and 57th regiments, and Lieutenant-General Hoang Xuan Lam's conduct. The presence of the Vietnamese Marine Division staff and Lieutenant-General Le Nguyen Khang provided only a backdrop to these events, and even the US Army belatedly recognized the Marines' drive for division status was correct and valuable.

First Regional Advisory Command's Major-General Howard Cooksey put forward at year's end that: "The Vietnamese Marine Division victory in Quang Tri City and its tactical excellence sets it apart from, and above other comparable units," and that "its distinctive performance and heroic conduct" deserved recognition. At last, the American Embassy in Saigon acknowledged the following: "Marine units recaptured Quang Tri City on September 16, 1972, after its abandonment by ARVN troops in May 1972." In recognition of this, US Ambassador Ellsworth Bunker and the commanding general of USMACV Army General Frederick C. Weyand proposed a US Presidential Unit Citation for the Vietnamese Marine Division. It was never approved.[17]

VICTORY LOST, 1973–75

With the ceasefire and withdrawal of American forces from South Vietnam in March 1973, Marine Advisory Unit logistical and advisory functions were turned over to the VNMC Logistics Support Branch (LSB) of the Navy Division of the Defense Attaché Office. This marked the end of an era of American advisory efforts with the Vietnamese Marines, but their Vietnamese counterparts and comrades were not forgotten. Marine Division expansion continued through 1973, reaching a peak of 939 officers and 14,290 men at the time of withdrawal of the final Americans. This figure later grew to more than 15,000 men. The Vietnamese Marines remained committed to the defense of the DMZ through 1974. To face the military crisis in 1975, three additional infantry battalions (14th, 16th, 18th) and a fourth brigade (468) formed in time for the South Vietnamese defeat.

First ordered to protect Hue and then Da Nang from the communist attack in spring 1975, the Marines were hastily pulled out with the collapse of the South Vietnamese in the northern provinces. Lieutenant-Colonel Anthony Lukeman, chief of the VNMC LSB, reported that Brigade 147 lost

17 The Vietnamese Marine Division received a US Army Valorous Unit Award, along with the 2d, 4th, and 9th Marine battalions.

The Vietnamese Marine Corps monument in Saigon honored its dead and wounded over the years since 1954. It was destroyed after the 1975 communist victory. This change of recognition did not make a difference to the historical record during its existence. (USMC)

80 percent of its men as it attempted to pull out of Hue City. "Other units experienced their most serious losses during the withdrawal from Da Nang, in which most of the Marines who were able to get aboard ships did so by swimming. Many Marines drowned in the attempt, or were killed on the beaches, and others who could not swim undoubtedly were captured." Five battalion commanders and some 40 company commanders died during the fighting. The division reorganized and deployed its remaining forces at Long Binh for the final battle of Saigon. There it stayed through the subsequent fighting at the end of April 1975. At that point, the Vietnamese Marine Corps ceased to exist except in memory and history. For the Vietnamese, the conflict was the end of a 30-year civil war in which the VNMC played a part until the bitter end.

THE BATTLEFIELD TODAY

The main Vietnamese military museums are located in Hanoi, while American Marine and Army museums are just south of Washington, DC. The locations of the fighting described can be visited by traveling along National Highway (QL) 1, to include Dong Ha, Quang Tri, Hue, and Da Nang. Going from the coastal plain further west requires more effort. Obvious military wreckage was scavenged for reuse. After nearly 50 years, the natural landscape and civilization have reclaimed the battlefields, together with new bridges. Vietnam is open to tourists and there are local and regional cultural landmarks to be seen, including a rebuilt Quang Tri Citadel. For those desiring a military focus, established tourism groups can be used, for example American Military Historical Tours, Incorporated (www.miltours.com) which has been conducting well-organized World War II, Korean War, and Vietnam Conflict visits since 1987. It is veteran owned and operated. Colonel John Ripley was one of their subject matter experts.

BIBLIOGRAPHY

Sources

Primary American sources are the *Senior Marine Advisor, Marine Advisory Unit Historical Summary 1972*, dated February 20, 1973; *Vietnamese Marine Corps/Marine Advisory Unit Historical Summary, 1953–1973*, dated March 22, 1973; *Center for Naval Analyses Study 1016, Documentation and Analysis of US Marine Corps Activity in Southeast Asia, 1972*, dated February 28, 1974; *US Marine Corps Command and Staff College, Easter Offensive Symposium, Course Material*, dated December 4, 1986. Other sources include Senior Marine Advisor (SMA), Marine Advisory Unit (MAU), and Vietnamese Marine Corps (VNMC) documents or oral histories held by the Marine Corps Historical Center Archive (MCHC), the Gray Research Center Archive (GRC), and the Marine Corps History Division (HD) at Quantico, VA, and are used with permission. Selected documents on both the topic of the Vietnamese Marines and the US Marine Advisory Unit are published in the occasional paper *Marine Advisors: With the Vietnamese Marine Corps* (Quantico: History Division, 2009). Other documentation includes the USMACV, *The Nguyen Hue Offensive, 7 January 1973* and BDM Corporation, *A Study of the Strategic Lessons Learned in Vietnam: Operational Analyses*, dated March 20, 1980. The official histories for the 1954–75 period are the multi-authored volumes *US Marines in Vietnam* (Washington, DC: Headquarters, US Marine Corps, 1977–97).

South Vietnamese accounts include Lieutenant-General Ngo Quang Truong, *The Easter Offensive of 1972* (Washington, DC: USA Center for Military History, 1979); General Cao Van Vien, *Leadership* (Washington, DC: USA Center for Military History, 1981); Brigadier-General Nguyen Duy Hinh, *Lam Son 719* (Washington, DC: USA Center for Military History, 1979); and Lieutenant-General Le Nguyen Khang, oral history interview, dated September 30, 1975 (Washington, DC: USMC History and Museum Division). North Vietnamese sources include People's Army of Vietnam Military Institute, *Vietnam: The Anti-U.S. Resistance War, 1954–1975* (Hanoi: PAVN Publishing House, 1980); Nguyen Khac Vien (ed.), *Indochina: The 1972–1973 Turning Point* (Hanoi: Xunhasaba, 1974); PAVN Senior Military Academy, "Quang Tri-Thua Thien Offensive Campaign," in *Collection of Sketches of Battles* (Hanoi: Ministry of Defense, 1986), pp. 18–19; and Colonel-General Van Tien Dung, "Some Problems Concerning the Art of Military Campaigns of the Vietnamese People's War," *People's Army Magazine* (Hanoi, December 1973), pp. 61–65; as translated by Robert J. Destatte.

Bibliography and further reading

Andrade, Dale, *America's Last Vietnam Battle: Halting the 1972 Easter Offensive* (Lawrence: University Press of Kansas, 2001)

Clarke, Jeffrey J., *Advice and Support: The Final Years, 1965–1973* (Washington, DC: USA Center for Military History, 1978)

Croizat, Victor J., *The Brown Water Navy: The River and Coastal War in Indo-China and Vietnam, 1948–1972* (New York: Blandford Press, 1985)

Daddis, Gregory A., *Withdrawal: Reassessing America's Final Years in Vietnam* (New York: Oxford University Press, 2017)

Emerson, Stephen, *North Vietnam's 1972 Easter Invasion* (Barnsley: Pen & Sword, 2020)

Fox, Wesley L., *Marine Rifleman: Forty-three Years in the Corps* (Washington, DC: Potomac Books, 2002)

Grandolini, Albert, *The Easter Offensive, Vietnam 1972: Invasion across the DMZ* (Solihull: Helion & Company, 2015)

Ha Mai Viet, *Steel and Blood: South Vietnamese Armor and the War for Southeast Asia* (Annapolis: Naval Institute Press, 2008)

Hunt, Richard A., *Melvin Laird and the Foundation of the Post-Vietnam Military, 1969–1973* (Washington, DC: Office of the Secretary of Defense, 2015)

Martin, Michael N., *Warriors of the Sea: Marines of the Second Indochina War* (Paducah: Turner Publishing, 2001)

Melson, Charles D. and Arnold, Curtis G., *US Marines in Vietnam: The War That Would Not End 1971–1973* (Washington, DC: History and Museums Division, 1991)

Melson, Charles D. and Renfrow, Wanda J. (eds.), *Marine Advisors: With the Vietnamese Marine Corps* (Quantico: History Division, 2009)

Miller, John G., *The Bridge at Dong Ha* (Annapolis: Naval Institute Press, 1989)

——, *The Co-Vans: US Marine Advisors in Vietnam* (Annapolis: Naval Institute Press, 2000)

Military History Institute of Vietnam (trans. Merle L. Pribbenow), *Victory in Vietnam: The Official History of the People's Army of Vietnam, 1954–1977* (Lawrence: University Press of Kansas, 2002)

Sorley, Louis (ed.), *Vietnam Chronicles: The Abrams Tapes, 1968–1972* (Lubbock: Texas Tech University, 2004)

Stoffey, Robert E., *Fighting to Leave: The Final Years of America's War in Vietnam, 1972–1973* (Minneapolis: Zenith Press, 2008)

Turley, Gerald H., "Time of Change in Modern Warfare," *Marine Corps Gazette*, December 1974, pp. 16–20

——, *The Easter Offensive* (Novato: Presidio Press, 1985)

Turley, Gerald H. and Wells, M.R., "Easter Invasion, 1972," *Marine Corps Gazette*, March 1973, pp. 18–29

Vietnamese Marines prepare to board a Boeing CH-46 Sea Knight helicopter provided by the 9th Marine Amphibious Brigade for the *Song Than* operations. (USMC)

ACRONYMS

ANGLICO	air–naval gunfire liaison company
ARVN	Army of the Republic of Vietnam
CTZ	corps tactical zone
DMZ	demilitarized zone separating North and South Vietnam at the 17th Parallel
DRVN	Democratic Republic of Vietnam (North Vietnam)
FRAC	First Regional Advisory Command
FSB	Fire Support Base
LAW/LAAW	light anti-tank or anti-armor weapon
LCC	amphibious command ship
LCM	landing craft mechanized
LSB	Logistics Support Branch
MATA	Military Assistance Training Advisor (Course)
MR	military region
NLF	National Liberation Front
NVA	North Vietnamese Army (US term for PAVN)
PAVN	People's Army of Vietnam (North Vietnam)
PLAF	People's Liberation Armed Forces
PF	Provincial Force
QL	*Quoc Lo* (national road, or highway)
RF	Regional Force
RVNAF	Republic of Vietnam Armed Forces (to include ARVN, VNN, VNAF)
USAF	US Air Force
USMACV	US Military Advisory Command, Vietnam
USMC	US Marine Corps
VC	Viet Cong (Vietnamese Communists)
VNAF	Vietnamese Air Force (Republic of Vietnam)
VNMC	Vietnamese Marine Corps (Republic of Vietnam)
VNN	Vietnamese Navy (Republic of Vietnam)

Loaded 9th Marine Amphibious Brigade CH-46 Sea Knight helicopters take off. Landing zones were improvised using available rural roadways. (USMC)

INDEX

Page references in **bold** refer to illustrations and numbers in brackets are caption locators.